T0208601

Valley of the Shadow

a journey through grief

Sybil Austin Skakle

iUniverse, Inc.
New York   Bloomington

Valley of the Shadow
a journey through grief

Copyright © 2009 Sybil Austin Skakle

iUniverse books may be ordered through booksellers or by contacting:

iUniverse
1663 Liberty Drive
Bloomington, IN 47403
www.iuniverse.com
1-800-Authors (1-800-288-4677)

Because of the dynamic nature of the Internet, any Web addresses or links contained in this book may have changed since publication and may no longer be valid. The views expressed in this work are solely those of the author and do not necessarily reflect the views of the publisher, and the publisher hereby disclaims any responsibility for them.

ISBN: 978-1-4401-3413-5 (pbk)
ISBN: 978-1-4401-3415-9 (cloth)
ISBN: 978-1-4401-3414-2 (ebk)

Printed in the United States of America

iUniverse rev. date: 6/19/09

Valley of the Shadow went through numerous revisions, which improved it. My perspective changed over the years. I need to acknowledge some dear friends who read the first manuscript- Irene Ferguson, Rudy Koster, Eleanor Wiles, Mary Johnson, Nancy Bennett. Their comments and reactions encouraged me to continue. I have had misgivings about including the chapter on sexuality. Nora Esthimer agreed to read and comment. Her remarks helped me decide that it was too important to delete. My niece and editor, Beth Williams asked me questions about vague references and edited my copy. I am grateful to all of them.

GRIEF BEGUN

With no goodbyes,
You died last month
Unexpectedly!

Death interrupted
Our shaping by God
And by one another

Questions bombard.
Memories flood.
Silence reigns.

Memory has no body
Nor does it speak.
I am lost and lonely

And angry over
Alienations
And wasted days

Sybil Austin Skakle

Contents

Dedicated to the memory of my husband

DONALD EDMUND SKAKLE, SR.

father of three sons:
Edmund, Andrew, Clifford

University of North Carolina, Chapel Hill
tennis coach and physical educator
1958-1980

Introduction

When I read Catherine Marshall's *To Live Again*, I did not know the reality of a husband's death. When I read Lynn Caine's *Widow*, I did know that reality. Caine's character, story, and circumstances were different from Marshall's and from mine. Reactions and resolutions have similarities. However, each story is separate and distinct. My book does not tell how to overcome grief. Rather it is the story of the first two years after my husband's death.

Readers will share my grief experiences and may learn something of value. While my ability to tell my story is important, the right receptivity is critical for acceptance of my efforts and any reward found by a reader.

Writing acted as a catharsis. However, I hope others will be helped by sharing my story. Perhaps those who doubt themselves and their ability to handle their grief will relate to mine and be convinced that what he or she is feeling is okay and prosper in other areas of their lives. Perhaps they will, as I did, discover that both failures and victories comprised grief work; that it is possible to be quite cheerful, in spite of tragedy and loss.

Pathos and praise happen! My despair sometimes seemed deeper than any I had known; worship sometimes sweeter than

I had ever experienced before, when God's Holy Spirit comforted me. There were times when I went through the motions of worship without feeling either joy or hope. I rejoiced from obedience. I served through habit. I breathed involuntarily.

A dear cousin of mine gave me a book she hoped would help, in the early days of my loss. The author said grief would make me a better person. I resented that author's assumption. The price required to become a better person seemed too high and the process too painful to accept. However, having arrived on the other side of grief, I am a better person and more compassionate. Grief equipped me to understand others who grieve, because I experience grief. However, no sane person would willingly choose the exacting discipline of grief.

I became more honest before God. I learned to trust him more. His promises became my lifeline in desperation's ocean. I learned the meaning of agape'—to love without strings. Because I grieved, I know better how to walk in faith without knowing where my next step leads. Grief helped me better appreciate God's loving patience

My grief journey covered many miles, literally and emotionally. You will see that my safe trip had both detours and roadblocks.

As I counted off the days, I wanted the pain to end. I hoped each new day would be better than the day before. I wanted improvement sooner than it came. I longed to arrive at a place in my feelings when my defenselessness gave way to assurance. However, many days would pass before I realized any true difference. My story reaches backward and forward in time, as I sought to come to terms with the issues that were a critical part of my grief journey and my life.

My advice to travelers en route is: be patient with yourself and your progress. Rejoice in little advances or none at all. Refuse guilt, because God invalidated it at Calvary. All those things you regret that you might have done are dregs in your cup. Wash them away with your tears and fill your cup with happy remembrances. Refuse to compare your progress with the progress of others.

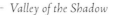

Your judgment is not dependable while you grieve. Value your uniqueness and play to your strengths. You are one of a kind! Reach out to others who need you. Let others help you. Accept their kindnesses as gifts of love from God. We are placed here to help one another. Others need us and we need others.

Sybil Austin Skakle

Sybil Bernadine Austin- university student
the girl Don Skakle married February 7, 1947

CHAPTER I

The Journey Begins

That Friday morning, when I entered the hospital pharmacy for work, Linda, the secretary of the department, stopped me. "Mrs. Skakle, your brother-in-law in Winston-Salem just called. He asks that you call him right away."

Why would Virgil, an anesthesiologist at Forsythe County Hospital in Winston-Salem, North Carolina, be calling me? Virgil Wilson and my youngest sister, Mona, were separated and anticipating a divorce.

Linda gave me the number and I went into an adjoining room to make the call. Virgil answered the phone right away. "Sybil, your sister is having a very bad time!"

I knew Mona had been having a hard time with their separation. With my heart in my throat, I asked, "What is wrong with Mona, Virgil?"

"She found Don dead in bed this morning," he answered.

I don't remember if I asked him any questions. I don't remember that he told me any details. I don't remember.

"Don't drive home alone," he cautioned.

"I'm all right!" I said, believing I was. I felt nothing.

I went into Linda's office and sat down beside her desk. "Mrs. Skakle, is something wrong?" she asked.

"Am I white?" I asked. Why did she inquire? Did she know the news already?

"Yes, you are," she replied, as concern clouded her soft brown eyes and furrowed her brow, beneath her long, dark brown hair.

I paused, unable to say those awful words. "My brother-in-law has just told me that Don is dead, and I don't believe it," I said as the tears flooded my eyes and ran silently down my face.

How could Don be dead? How could Don, not yet fifty-seven, be dead? Both his grandmothers had lived past ninety. His parents, as well as mine, had made three score and ten. It had been less than a year since his father, Stanley Gordon Skakle, age eighty-five, had died. Don would not be fifty-seven until June. Virgil had just told me that Don died in his sleep at my sister's home. How could it be? We thought we had lots of time. We expected to celebrate our golden wedding anniversary. Don had not been ill. He was in good health. It was April 18, 1980, the day of the Atlantic Coast Conference Tennis Tournament, and he had gone to Winston-Salem for it yesterday. How could Don be dead?

I had planned to pick up my luggage at home in Chapel Hill and head west as soon as I finished work at Durham County Hospital pharmacy. The anticipation of being with Mona to share the rest of the tournament with Don and the members of the tennis team had filled my mind until now.

Don and I had planned to stay at the motel with the players. Something happened after our first reservations were confirmed that required Don to make new ones, at another motel. There were not enough rooms to accommodate Don and me at the new one. It was then that I called Mona to ask if we might stay with her. That is why Mona found Don that morning instead of me. Someone commented, "Sybil, your sister saved you from that."

Dazed, I walked into the main part of the pharmacy. Several staff members gathered around me. It seemed everyone knew what had happened. Their hugs and efforts to comfort me showed they cared. One of the young pharmacy technicians asked, "Mrs. Skakle, can I get you a cup of coffee and a cigarette?"

Touched by her concern, I smiled and declined. She offered me her comfort—a cigarette and cup of coffee. These were not mine.

Others made decisions for me. The director of pharmacy services, Gerald Stahl, would drive my car to my home in Chapel Hill, and Bill Martin, his assistant, would drive me home. I felt strange and disconnected. What was there to talk about? Nothing seemed worth words. I don't remember anything we said to one another, only that we made an effort at conversation.

Shortly after we arrived at the house, a longtime friend from my church, Dot Reynolds, arrived, and Mr. Stahl and Bill took their leave. Dot said she had heard the news on the early morning radio.

I had been listening to the radio, to my favorite inspirational station, which I usually turned to on my ride to work each day. The message and soothing music usually prepared me for the day. Where might I have been when the announcement was made? What did they say? If I had heard it, what might I have done?

Other friends arrived. The phone began to ring. I received the people, while others answered the phone and the door. At first, I thought I would need to go to Winston-Salem. I felt torn. Somehow, I've always thought that I should have gone to the hospital. When they took me into the room of the hospital, wherever it was, I would have said: "Don, get up. The tennis team is waiting for you."

Somehow, I feel that I failed to live up to my faith in Christ Jesus by not going. Somehow, I failed Don by not going to Winston-Salem to see him that morning. Jesus had said in John 14:12: "He that believeth on me, the works that I do shall he do also, and greater works than these shall he do; because I go unto the Father."

Christ arose from the dead and had brought Lazarus back to life after three days. Yet, I stayed home to receive visitors, thinking that I should be on my way to Winston- Salem and to Forsythe County Hospital to show a doubting world that Christ Jesus is alive and working in the lives of men. Might unswerving faith have changed the outcome of the story from that day forward? Someday I will know. Someday I will understand why Don died.

Our three sons had to be located. Don's brother, Gordon, and his family, and their stepmother, Beth, in Massachusetts needed to know. My sisters: Margie Newton in Greensboro; Jo Oden in Hatteras; and RubyAustin, my brother's widow, also in Hatteras, needed to be notified. I do not know who made all those calls. Maybe Kathey, married to my oldest son, Eddie, for she had heard the news that morning as she drove toward Asheville for an education meeting. She immediately turned around to return to Chapel Hill and soon arrived at the house.

Whoever called to locate Andy, son number two, found him in Charleston, South Carolina. He and his dog Toasty left the week before for Andy to play tennis in the Southern Tennis Circuit, beginning in Shreveport, Louisiana. They were traveling in our green Plymouth Valiant. Someone decided Andy should fly home. Someone ordered tickets for him and arranged to pick him up at the airport. After the tournament ended, another tournament player from North Carolina brought the car and Toasty home.

My sister, Jo, told me that she had been the one to tell Eddie. He was not at his home in Hatteras. A commercial fisherman, he was fishing out of Wanchese, North Carolina, located in upper Dare County on Roanoke Island at the time. She left a message for him and asked that he return her call as soon as he received it. When he called, she told him the sad news. He piled his stuff in the back of his truck and headed west on Route 64, toward Chapel Hill.

Clifford, our youngest son, was playing tennis for a private club team in Aix-en-Provence, France. Due to the language barrier and the difficulty with the overseas communication network, he could not be reached immediately. Finally, they managed to make the connection, possibly at 3 AM in France, and someone said Cliff was expected later.

Bill Cobey, head of the University of North Carolina Athletic Department, came to offer condolences. He leaned forward in his chair, his voice and facial features full of concern. Don, he said, had recently visited him and had shared for the first time his frustration with his position as both coach and physical educator. "I wish he had talked to me sooner," he said.

Dr. W. S. Joyner, who had been our family physician since we arrived in Chapel Hill in 1958, called to ask questions and express concern and regrets. He advised that I should agree to the autopsy that had been requested. It might provide information that could be important for our sons' medical histories. Of course, I agreed.

Two years later, I learned that Don's grandfather, John A. Skakle, had died in a similar way in 1920. His grandfather had come home for lunch from Plymouth Cordage Company in Plymouth, Massachusetts, laid down for his usual short nap after lunch, and never awakened. Had Don known this, would he have thought to question the circumstances of his grandfather's death and possibly prevented his own? I doubt it!

The difference between medical practice in 1920 and 1980 is too great to imagine. Even in 1980, neither doctors nor the public, knew the extent of damage caused by stress on the human body. People vary widely in their tolerance of stress. As far as I know, Don did not know the story of his grandfather's death. We would never have suspected a genetic link that might have warned us of danger. Possibly the cause of the 1920 death of his sixty-year-old grandfather and Don's were the same.

Except for taking a daily five-milligram dose of Zaroxlyn, for slightly elevated blood pressure, Don was in good health. He took a Kinised tablet, prescribed for a stomach ulcer, as needed to aid digestion. Kinised contained a small dose of Phenobarbital in its formulation. The medical examiner, who did the autopsy, questioned me about the presence of Phenobarbital, but explained that it had not been significant in his death. Though present, it was too small to have caused death, even when combined with the alcohol in the drink he had shared with Mona after he came to her house on Thursday evening.

His autopsy report revealed no identifiable cause of death. There was no heart damage. No blood clots. No hemorrhage had occurred. The death certificate reads: "Possible arrhythmia." He went to bed dog-tired and did not awaken when the alarm went off the next morning.

Those who reported on the events of Thursday night, when the coaches vied for advantages for their players in the tournament draws, said the meeting was lengthy. One coach remarked that Don had been quieter than usual that evening. Mona said it was almost midnight when Don arrived at her home. He spoke of "dragging butt!" I had waited until after midnight for his usual call to me, which never came.

Don had been a varsity tennis player at Carolina between 1945 and 1950. His singles record, 60–1. His only loss, a default, caused by illness, spoiled his perfect singles tournament record. Flu defeated him, and he had to leave the court in the middle of his match. While he coached at Carolina, twenty-two years, his teams captured 18 of 20 Atlantic Coast Conference titles.

Don Skakle did not meet his team at 8:30 AM on April 18, 1980. He did not witness how gallantly they played, in spite of the loss of their coach. He did not experience the pain and disappointment of having Carolina drop to fifth place in the Atlantic Coast Conference in 1980. Don would not come home again to me.

Don Skakle and one of his winning tennis teams, circa 1970

The Chapel Hill Newspaper

The Chapel Hill Newspaper   Sunday, April 20, 1980

Skakle Expected The Best And Was Able To Get It

Don Skakle paced nervously from one singles court to another two weeks ago watching North Carolina's tennis players compete in an important Atlantic Coast Conference match.

The man whom everyone calls "Coach" stood with crossed arms while he watched one of his players work his opponent out of position then slam a sure winner squarely into the net.

Skakle kicked the ground with his foot and shook his head, and the creases in his tanned face became a little deeper.

"He'd be winning if he was playing like he AND I know he can," Skakle grumbled.

Skakle expected only the best performances from his players, and when the UNC tennis coach died Friday in Winston-Salem at age 56, he left a legacy that is a tribute to his fierce determination to mold winners out of the netmen of UNC.

With a man like Skakle, it can be difficult to pinpoint the secret for tremendous success that included a 416-51 record in his 22 years as head coach at UNC, but a type of success that went much deeper than wins and losses.

When Skakle recruited, his main selling point was the strong academic tradition at UNC. Secondary in his sales pitch was the 16 ACC titles and two ties for the title which UNC accumulated under him.

HIS MOST fervent wishes were that his players be gentlemen on the court and give every ounce of effort they could muster.

"They didn't play if they didn't play up to their potential," says Fred Rawlings, one of Skakle's players in the late 1960s who won two ACC championships in fifth flight singles and now is a club pro in Roanoke, Va.

"The 110 percent was expected of you and he didn't put up with any foolishness on the court," Rawlings says. "Teams always were tough under Coach because when he coached you, he led you to believe that only through hard work would they be winners."

Pride, dedication and determination were key elements in Skakle's formula of success and he had

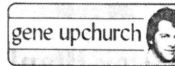

gene upchurch

occasional tiffs with players who weren't willing to do their darndest or shed that extra drop of sweat to win.

"The levels of everybody's games improved while they were playing for Skakle," Rawlings says.

Skakle's determination and the determination of his teams produced tremendous results. In eighteen of Skakle's 22 years, the Tar Heels won the ACC championship. Two teams (1965 and 1970) went undefeated and seven others lost but a single match.

"He brought out the best in his players," Rawlings says. "He was an awfully good coach, especially at putting together teams. The doubles teams he put together always jelled and he always managed to find guys who really wanted to play tennis."

While his teams produced remarkable records, Skakle himself amassed some laurels: a member of the U.S. Olympic Tennis Committee, a District III coach of the year and a finalist for national coach of the year.

Yet, whenever he was asked him what satisfied him the most, he always said that he got more satisfaction from working with his players than anything else.

"Every one of the players loved him," Rawlings says. "He was like a father to all of us."

On the back cover of the UNC tennis brochure is an adaptation by Skakle of a poem, a few lines of which help explain what Skakle thought was his purpose as the UNC tennis coach:

". . . Coach them, I pray, not in the paths of ease and comfort, but under the stress and spur of difficulties and challenges. Here let them learn to stand up in the storm; here let them learn compassion for those who fail . . ."

This article originally appeared in *The Chapel Hill News.*

CHAPTER II

The Players Gather

Kathey was the first of the family to arrive at the house, which was already full of people. Friends came to visit and to bring food. Our next-door neighbor, a restaurateur who had never been in our house before that day, provided coffee for days afterward. People are so good. One friend from church took me into my bedroom and urged me to relax and try to sleep, but I could not sleep.

Eddie arrived by the time Virgil brought Mona to the house that afternoon. When I met Mona, she was crying as she enfolded me into her arms. Strangely, I remained dry-eyed. I suppose that was what they call shock. Did I believe I was having a bad dream?

I was lying on the couch in the living room when Andy answered the phone in the wee hours of the morning of April 19 and called me to the phone to talk to Cliff. Someone sent a telegram to Cliff after he could not be reached by phone and requested he call his mother. He told us later that the phone went dead right after I spoke. All he had heard was that his father had died. He did not know how, when, where, or why, and he had no change to feed the telephone.

"Mom, I kept thinking you must have awakened and found Dad dead beside you," he said. "I worried about you."

Nothing I might have said over the phone would have been

enough. I remember the stricken look of a young junior tennis player, staying with us during state competition, when we awakened him to tell him his father had died--even though Bruce knew his father was very ill and dying. Cliff probably looked like Bruce did that night. Cliff had lost his father, his coach, and his best friend. Nothing I could have said would have helped. My arms around him might have helped him and me, but an ocean separated us.

(Cliff remembers those in Aix en Provence who shared those first terrible minutes with him. In 2003, Cliff and his daughter Danielle went back to visit those friends.)

When Cliff arrived, after that long airplane flight, he stood in the middle of the living room looking dazed and lost. Beth Skakle called me aside. "Sybil, dear, you need to take Cliff into your room and be alone with him."

In my state of mind, with so many people around, I did not know what I should do from one minute to the next. I followed Beth's direction, and when Cliff and I were alone, the door closed, he buried his head in my lap and sobbed like a brokenhearted child. I was grateful that Beth prompted me to take him aside.

Later, Eddie, Andy, Cliff and I went to view Don's body at Walker's Funeral Home. When Cliff approached the body of his father, his knees buckled and Andy and Eddie caught him. Don had reacted similarly one Sunday evening in 1968 when his father called from Florida to tell him that his mother had died of a massive stroke. His father and mother had returned home after attending church. She collapsed as they started into the house and never regained consciousness. Don's reaction was like a hard blow to the solar plexus when his father told him his mother was dead. His knees nearly went out from under him.

Eddie looked at the corpse and said, "He's not there!"

Eddie was right. Don was not there. That which he had left behind, dressed in his Carolina blue suit, looked like him. However, the hard, cold statue that looked like who he had been, without animation and personality, was not him. Don was not there!

Andy said, "That might be me someday."

His saying that registered in my consciousness and acted like a red flag. I wondered about that "someday." What a strange statement for a young, healthy, twenty-eight-year-old male. What was he thinking? The death of his father was his third recent emotional blow. His marriage had failed and he had lost his job. How was he managing?

Andy made himself scarce around the premises, perhaps seeking resources within himself to survive. Perhaps the friends in his life at that time helped him cope.

Eddie seemed confident that he could handle the situation. "As the oldest brother, I felt I had to be strong and courageous and maintain optimism," he later said.

Eddie faces life's difficulties, as he did even as a little boy, with confidence that he is capable of handling anything that comes his way, although it is God's mercy that as a child he was not mangled by dogs or kidnapped by some predator when he adventured away from home. His commercial fishing boat nearly broke apart under him in the current of Hatteras Inlet, while he fished alone.

Probably no one expected me to be coherent and in control. I felt I had a role to play in the events that were unfolding and sought to keep my composure. I suppose I expected everyone else to listen for their cues and to do their parts. I had to handle my own lines. I thank God for the built-in ability of the human psyche to survive emotional shock. Denial is a strange emotion, but it helps us live through the disasters that might otherwise destroy us.

———— C H A P T E R   I I I ————

People Who Need People

Barbra Streisand sang: "People who need people are the luckiest people in the world." I needed all those people who reached out to me. Perhaps those people needed to reach out because they were, also, people who need people. Many relatives and friends phoned to let my sons and me know that they cared that we were hurting. Some knew Don well and shared our loss. Other telephone calls surprised me. One came from an old Massachusetts classmate of Don's, another from my niece's former mother-in-law, and another from a sports writer from *The Durham Herald*, whom I suspected of calling more out of curiosity than from compassion, which may have been untrue. He may have known Don well and been greatly affected by his death.

People seek to comfort someone for their own reasons. Some, especially the uninitiated, do so out of duty. Some fear they have no words to express their regret. They have not learned that words are less important than their presence and love. Some are better with words than others are. Paul in 1 Corinthians 1:7 explains that those who have suffered are those best able to console.

The effectiveness of a support group, whether the sufferer is bereaved, overweight, alcoholic, or addicted to food or gambling, is dependent on the empathy of the members who have personal knowledge of the struggle. Those who have suffered similarly have been equipped. It is not "right words." Hugs and tears will minister when words seem inadequate and superfluous. When someone is bereaved, it is sufficient that someone cares enough to make an effort to console—to be present.

Besides telephone calls and visits there were letters, cards, flowers, telegrams, food, and favors. Every act of kindness seemed special to me. Months afterward, I had not finished writing notes to express my appreciation.

Several weeks afterward, Jo at Hatteras told me friends asked her if I had received their flowers. No, I had not forgotten to write. Their flowers had not arrived. I wrote to tell them of my appreciation and to assure them that their flowers meant less than that they cared and were thinking of me. I contacted the florist and requested their money be refunded, but never knew if that request was honored. Flowers wilt, but memories of thoughtfulness do not fade.

The task of note writing had its function. It put me in touch with those who felt poorer for Don's death. Some of their notes gave me back a part of Don's life that I had missed. Stories some people shared about him fed a deep need to know how others thought and felt about him. Their communications told me that they held him in high regard. The many expressions of condolence were huge.

When we talked to Wallace Womble, the funeral director, I expressed a wish to have a closed casket. He said, "Mrs. Skakle, I hope you will reconsider. So many people knew Don Skakle."

Yes, I remembered. Don had told me about one student who asked for an appointment. As it turned out, the student had not come to discuss the class he had with Don, but his studies in another area of UNC. The student was oblivious to Don's sacrifice in granting him time from his crowded schedule.

Don told me about a student couple, pregnant and scared, who came to see him. They made an appointment with him to ask what they should do. He asked the simplest question: "Do you love each other?"

They answered in the affirmative and Don told them what they should have already known: "Tell your folks right away. They will understand and help you to get married quickly."

He and I were close enough to our student days to understand their anxiety. We remembered how much grief we made for ourselves by marrying secretly, not because anyone objected. We wanted the privileges of marriage sooner than our planned date in September, so we married in February, planning on a second ceremony, that others might share, when September came.

Moreover, I remembered my anxiety when I found myself pregnant nine months later. Still in school, I asked Dean Jacobs of Pharmacy School if it would be possible for me to continue. He replied, "We're all adults here, Sybil. Of course you may continue."

We needed advice from people with more experience than we had. That Christmas, we told his mother and dad, all of us standing together in the middle of their kitchen in Waltham, Massachusetts. His mother and father laughed happily and embraced us. We had no reason to be afraid. They were in our rooting section.

The couple Don advised to marry took his advice. Wherever they are, whoever they are, I hope they have lived happily ever after.

Don counseled many young people, for various reasons: from those he taught in physical education classes and those he coached on the University of North Carolina tennis teams to church school classes. Seemingly, many felt close enough to him to seek his help. He put himself out for others. Now, I thought, no one can hurt him or demand too much of him ever again.

However, when I remembered how people made calls on his time and how generously he responded, I reconsidered. I did not insist on having a closed casket. In fact, he had no casket at all!

I had read that undertakers try to sell costly caskets to the bereaved. I do not remember making a decision to not have a casket or if anyone tried to sell us one. Perhaps I did take part in the decision. Certainly, there was no need for a casket. Our sons and I decided on cremation. (I had told Don I favored cremation. He did not object, so I concluded that his silence gave me his consent to make that decision.)

The evening before the memorial service, we were available to friends and acquaintances at the funeral home, where Don's corpse lay on a stretcher. White socks were on his feet. His glasses were on his face. Don was a frugal man, and we never tried to live beyond our means or rely on status symbols. However, later I thought how strange it seemed to see his body lying there like that. I had never seen a viewing done like that before. Did others wonder about it? Someone told me that we could have rented a casket for the viewing.

The Rev. Russell Stott, our minister, helped plan Don's beautiful memorial service. He gave each of our sons and me an opportunity to speak, as well as Don's colleagues and church and tennis friends. The service included joyous music, one of which was Don's favorite: "Count Your Blessings."

Comforted by the Scripture, the testimonies, and the music, Cliff put his arm around my shoulder and smiled, as he had not done since he arrived from Europe. Mr. Womble had considerately agreed to delay releasing the body to the crematorium, especially for Cliff's sake. However, no one needed to go back to the funeral home. God's loving presence in the congregation had comforted our hearts.

Mr. Womble showed remarkable patience and kindness by not rushing us away after the memorial service. Even so, there were many people who neither my sons nor I were able to speak to personally, one, a former tennis team member, who arrived from Florida only in time for the memorial service. While aware of him and of others being there, we had no chance to speak to them. Haste robs the bereaved of the consolation they seek to offer and the bereaved have no opportunity to offer consolation to those who have come. Sometimes the service provides the only occasion to share the comfort of word or touch. With the linking person removed, the death of one mutually loved and respected gone, there is only that moment to share.

Some felt close enough to come by our home. Some may have been reluctant to presume on our privacy and hospitality. Some we never saw again. Others, with tight schedules, showed their respect and honor and were anxious to attend to their next obligations. The reception that friends or church families give nowadays provides an opportunity to share fellowship for those who need something more than the service.

When I die, I hope those I leave behind will celebrate my life without sadness. I trust that no one will be glad I am gone because I have been unkind. I look forward to reunion with those who preceded me to Heaven as Scripture promises. I expect to be singing with the angels and visiting with Jesus and those I loved on Earth.

Many gave gifts toward a proposed memorial garden, where Don's ashes were to be buried, at Amity United Methodist Church. People were generous, but the plan for the garden never became a reality. The money was redirected to other church projects -- to provide pulpit Bibles; to help pay for the baptismal font; to place a framed print, "Offer Them Christ," in the entrance hall of the church; and to help pay for a steeple for the church, where Don served variously as usher, church school teacher, and head of the administrative board from June 1959 until his death in 1980.

Mr. Womble assured me that the ashes would be safe in the funeral home until the family could get together for their dispersion or burial. That would not be until Thanksgiving weekend of 1982, and even then, Andy was missing. After Sunday worship at Hatteras United Methodist Church, available family members gathered at Oden's Cemetery with the Rev. Fred Roberts to have the interment service. All we needed was a post digger, which my brother-in-law Carlos Oden provided. After Eddie discovered Skakle misspelled on the grave marker provided by the United States government, we turned it over and I had it redone with the following inscription: "Write me as one who loves his fellow man," from Leigh Hunt's *Abou Ben Adam*. Don showed by his life his love for his fellow man. "May his tribe increase." Don loved and needed people.

We buried Don's ashes beside the graves of my parents and my father's forbearers, going back to the 1700s.

PSALM of SACRED PLACE
Oden Graveyard, Hatteras, N.C.

Praise God for all generations of my people.
Celebrate their lives now past.
Remember them in this place where their bones
and ashes lie,
On a sandy hill within the sound of the
mighty Atlantic.
Thank you, O God, for your faithfulness to them.
For protecting them during fearsome storms-
hurricanes and gales.
For your graciousness to them during the ebb and
flow of their lives' tides.
Establish this place as a sacred one for future
generations.
May we remember your steadfast love sustained
those before us,
And will protect us who trust you and obey
Jesus, your son.
When my ashes join my ancestors' and husband's,
My lips will praise you in the New Jerusalem.
Hallelujah! Amen.

CHAPTER IV

The Way it Was

Don's schedule was exhausting. His varsity tennis job, begun in 1958, had escalated from a spring sport to a year-round responsibility. Besides his position as varsity tennis coach at the University of North Carolina, he taught a full load in the required physical-education program. Dr. Carl Blythe headed the physical-education program; Bill Cobey acted as director of athletics. I like to think they would have made adjustments, to coordinate Don's coaching and teaching, had they realized. In trying to give each program all he believed his superiors expected of him, Don's reserves of time and energy were exhausted.

Recruiting during the 1979-80 year had been especially heavy. When a prospect visited the university, Don relied on one of the team members to share his room on campus. That did not always happen. It could be a hassle. Once I volunteered to have a young man stay at our home to relieve Don of some frustration. Opening our home to a recruit would have been easier any time; however, Atlantic Coast Conference rules forbade it. Prospects must be protected from "undue influence." We did what we had to do. The recruit stayed with us. We did not tell. Since the prospect decided to go to some other school, we were not guilty of having influenced him in favor of Carolina.

Professor Don and Sybil Skakle at a university function
circa 1959

Entertainment for the recruit consisted of a football game or a basketball game, depending on the season. Don or one of the scholarship team members would take the recruit to eat at the athletes' training table for the length of his stay.

There were additional responsibilities, which infringed on Don's time. Checking nets on all the tennis courts used by the general student body, as well as those used by the team, fell to his lot. Perhaps department budget made that necessary. I don't know why. One spring evening after supper, I went with him to check nets on UNC campus.

Ronald Pharr, the tennis team manager that year, helped with many tasks. However, Don took responsibility for the details related to away team trips; and the 1980 spring tennis schedule required a great deal of travel. Since the beginning of March, the team had a match, either at home or away, almost every day. I am not sure who was responsible for the number of matches scheduled. It may have been Don's own doing. It may have been dictated by the athletic department.

However, teaching and coaching were not the only reasons he was suffering stress. There were other emotional drains. Andy had taken a tennis professional job in 1978 in Kinston, North Carolina, where Don and I had spent a week in June 1979, setting up the furniture Andy's fiancée, Bonnie Johnson, had shipped to Kinston from Knoxville, Tennessee. We waxed floors and made small repairs to the house they had purchased in anticipation of their marriage. Don and I were a team. We worked well together and enjoyed our time with Andy; we found satisfaction in preparing the house for the arrival of Andy's bride-to-be.

Cliff took a tennis job near Atlantic City, New Jersey, that spring. Don taught the first session of summer school at the university. Don and I went to visit him, in July. While we were with him, Don had an early morning call from his brother Gordon in Florida, to tell him doctors had determined that their father's prostate cancer was advanced and scheduled surgery the following week. A second phone message the same day called us back to North Carolina. Kathey's mother, Ruth Hinton, had died of cancer. We cut short our visit with Cliff to return to North Carolina for Ruth's funeral, and following her funeral, Eddie, Kathey, Don and I drove to Winter Haven, Florida, to be with Gordon and his wife Caroline, who were visiting from Maine, and Poppa's wife Beth to await the outcome of Poppa's surgery. The prognosis was grim.

We came back to the motel after having seen Poppa. Don and I said goodnight to Eddie and Kathey and went to our room. Don was deeply troubled as we went to bed. "Dad's dying and I can't help him," he said, and began to cry. He turned toward me in the bed, I took him into my arms, and he buried his face into my shoulder. Had he ever been so vulnerable with me? That moment was one of the most tender of our thirty-three-year marriage.

Registration for fall classes at Carolina was under way August 23, 1979. Don, helping register students at Woolen Gymnasium, received word by phone that his father had died. We were planning to leave for Knoxville, Tennessee for the August 25 wedding of Bonnie and Andy. Invitations for their wedding were mailed weeks before. We, and others, agreed that the wedding should continue, while the family delayed Poppa's funeral until we could get there, after the wedding.

So, it was that Eddie and Kathey, Don and I drove to Knoxville, Tennessee, together. Cliff flew in from New Jersey. He had gone to sleep at the wheel of his red Mazda coming home to his apartment one night. He hit a pole, which broke, smashing his car and him in it. He spent three or four days in a hospital before he called to tell us what had happened to him. When he flew in for the wedding, his hair in front had still not grown out well. Andy drove to Knoxville alone, and Mona arrived by car from Winston-Salem.

Don and Sybil Skakle at rehearsal dinner August 24, 1979

After the rehearsal party ended, and all except our family had left the motel where we were staying, our family had our own party in the lounge. Don and I danced to the music, and he smiled into my eyes. He had not looked at me in that way for a long while. When I have since doubted my attractiveness as a woman, I remembered his eyes and his smile that night. They give me the confidence I need. Yes, Don loved me.

Eddie threw his arms around us as we danced and sang: "We Are Family." I begged him and Cliff not to keep Andy up all night, to be considerate of the fact that he was getting married the next day, Saturday.

Bonnie's divorced parents were both musicians and academicians. Bonnie's mother taught at the University of Tennessee in Knoxville and was excited about the beautiful musical program she had planned for her daughter's wedding. Don served as best man for Andy. Eddie and Cliff were his attendants, dressed in Carolina blue tuxedos. We were all so beautiful that we did not have time to think about our loss of Poppa Skakle. We put grief aside for two days, to take up again when the wedding festivities were over.

Andy and Bonnie left for Gatlinburg and their honeymoon. Cliff flew back to New Jersey. Eddie and Kathey put Don and me on the plane for Florida to attend Poppa Skakle's funeral, and they drove our car back to Chapel Hill.

By November, Bonnie had decided she wanted no more of her job in Kinston, N.C., which she disliked, and she and Andy were not getting along. She left to go home to Knoxville for Thanksgiving with no plan of returning.

Soon after, just before Christmas, Andy lost his job, left the house they had bought together, and came home to stay with us. Along the way, he had rescued puppies that someone had tried to drown. Only one survived the cold dunking, a light tan German shepherd, which Andy named Toasty.

Ultimately, the total investment that Bonnie, Andy, probably Bonnie's mother, and we made to keep the house was lost. The job market and the housing market were both in slump. Andy could not find a job in this area.

Cliff, Andy and Eddie all dressed up for the wedding
August 25, 1979

We made the payments as long as we could. A cat lived in the house, taking care of itself, until the day in February when Andy and Cliff went to Kinston to move the rest of Andy's things out of the house. Neither Andy nor I was equipped to handle the problem of the house. We allowed the former owner to repossess the house-- in much better shape than when Andy and Bonnie bought it. The cat got out while Andy and Cliff were moving stuff. Dogs caught and killed the cat. That too was part of the nightmare.

Christmas came and went. Cliff came home and brought his fiancée, Mary, from New Jersey. Eddie and Kathey came. In January, I celebrated my fifty-fourth birthday. In February, we had our thirty-third anniversary and drove to Norfolk, Virginia, to spend the weekend with my cousin, Minerva, and her husband Bill Johnson. We were alone for the first time in a very long time. Either I had been working or he had been away every weekend since school began. We did not talk much. For me, it was enough that we were together. Both of us had many thoughts and feelings to process as we rode along in the bright crisp day.

Minerva and Bill told me that Don talked to them about his dad the day after we arrived, while I slept off a migraine that did not let up all day long. While they went out to lunch and talked, I slept. My migraine may have had a purpose. Don had the Johnsons' whole attention and had a chance to talk about his dad and his loss.

After church and lunch on Sunday with our friends, Don and I returned to Chapel Hill and our schedules.

There had been one crisis after another in our personal lives, and there were losses and disappointments for Don in his academic career, as well. He did not get that prime recruit for the Carolina Tennis team. He had not succeeded in obtaining the indoor tennis courts for which he sought help from the athletic department and financial support and interest from former Carolina tennis people. He served two department heads, in two jobs, and yet the compensation he received was low, for the University required faculty members to do research and publish for advancement. Don did not have time to write. He did not have energy or desire to write. Don, an associate professor with no hope of advancement to full professor, believed teaching was the most important contribution he could make to the university and to his students. That is the way it was and it is the reason I believe stress killed my husband.

Chapter V

Ruminating

Over and over, I relived our last week together in my mind. I tried to understand why he died and I recalled earlier details of our lives. I remembered that Don honored my request, made before we came to Chapel Hill in August of 1958, to enter UNC graduate school and assume the position as North Carolina varsity tennis coach. We agreed to keep Sundays for worship and family. So, we attended church that last April Sunday morning. However, I spent much of the afternoon working on a program I was to present to United Methodist Women on Monday evening. Once, as I passed through the living room, Don said to me from the couch, "Leave it alone for a while. Come and sit down with me."

"I'm trying to learn the music so I can teach it to the others," I said.

"I've not heard you play the piano in a long while. I've enjoyed listening."

We both loved music, but I never played well. With only spotty training as a girl, between teachers, I learned bad fingering habits. Don's comment surprised me. Perhaps he missed the sound of home, which he had missed so much of that year.

On Monday, Don took my typed copy of the program with him to run off copies at Woollen Gymnasium, where he had his office. Mimeographing had shortened and blurred some of the words on the pages. (We easily make clean copies today with our word processors and printing machines.) He brought them to me that afternoon and had carefully corrected each mimeographed sheet. I knew he had probably made those corrections during the time he ate a sandwich in his office at lunchtime. "Oh, Honey, you didn't have time to do that for me," I said.

Tears welled up in his eyes. Startled, I went to him, put my arms around his waist and said, "Thank you, darling."

What was going on with Don? Why did he react that way? It could have been grief over his father. It could have been something else.

After supper, I went to the United Methodist Women meeting, gave the program and did not get home until after 10 PM.

On Tuesday night, Don and I watched a television special together. I sat on the left end of the couch, where the light was best, reading between segments of the show. Don got up from his chair across the room, stretched out on the couch and put his head in my lap. When had he ever done that? Why didn't we turn off the TV and talk? That is what we should have done.

On Wednesday, the Carolina tennis team met the Duke team at Durham. I stopped by the Duke courts from work at Durham General Hospital. The match play had been going on for some time. The competition, far from over, continued between the archrivals while a mild day turned chilly. Sitting in the stands, wrapped in Don's white wool blanket from his U.S. Coast Guard days, I still felt cold. Kathey, who taught distributive education in Manteo, North Carolina, sat watching with me briefly. She was staying overnight in Durham with an aunt and would continue her trip to Asheville for a work-related meeting the following morning. Don, wearing his Carolina blue spring jacket, stood on the bank watching the matches while the shift in temperature made that jacket inadequate.

Kathey left, and I decided I should leave also. I had choir practice at seven. And I wanted to leave so I could give Don his blanket. When I wrapped it around his shoulders and took my leave, he visibly shuddered as he gratefully hugged it close. Loyalty required that he support his players even if he froze in place.

It did not surprise me when he did not arrive home until after 10 PM. Responsibility to his team meant he would be sure all the tennis team fellows were fed before he left them. The Duke match had run beyond the serving time of the UNC Athletic Training Table. (Sometimes, when the matches ran late, he invited me to join them at Brady's on East Franklin Street in Chapel Hill. We enjoyed the oysters there.) When Don came in the house, he looked haggard.

Don and I had been in bed only a short while when the phone jarred us awake. The clock on the bedside table said 2:30 AM. The call did not surprise me. It was my night to answer calls from the nursing staff of Durham County Hospital for pharmacy service. Don, exhausted, offered to go with me. "No reason for both of us to lose our sleep," I said.

I resented that trip for one little blue pill, which happened to be Zaroxylyn, given for hypertension. It was so near to breakfast, just a few hours away, that I thought they might have waited until then. It seemed senseless. Imagine, if you will, how much that little pill cost someone.

It was 4 AM when I climbed back in bed. Don did not rouse. When the alarm went off, we ignored it to squeeze in a few more minutes of rest. The doorbell startled us awake. Neither of us had remembered that the representative for Jewel Tea Co. was due that morning. His visit kept both of us from being late for work.

Mr. Long had called on us for many years to sell coffee, tea, and a special salad dressing we liked. In later years, his catalogs tempted us to buy clothing and housewares. We had come to trust and appreciate him as a friend.

I rushed out the door and left Mr. Long and Don in the kitchen to complete the business transaction. (After Don's death, I asked Mr. Long, "Did I kiss Don before I left?" It was terribly important to me to have told him goodbye that last morning. "Yes, Mrs. Skakle, you did," he replied.)

The tennis team had to play a match that had been rained out the week before that Thursday morning. Don came home at lunchtime to pack for the road trip. Preparation required that he take care of many details besides his personal ones. Tasks included collecting clothing, rackets, tennis strings, cars, and money for the team expenses. While Don relied on the team manager for many things, he insisted on taking care of the incidentals himself.

I felt uneasy. Don had looked so gaunt the night before. How glad I would be when the Atlantic Coast Conference Tennis Tournament ended. Athletes and actors expect to sacrifice everything to their performances; and I observed the medical interns from Duke at Durham County Hospital with their demanding schedules. All of them must disregard their tiredness and continue to give of themselves. Don could not choose to take a day off and stay home in bed because he was tired and feeling on his last leg. I wondered how an intern on a twenty-four-hour shift could be alert enough in a critical emergency. Yet, like soldiers under fire on a battlefield, individual responsibility to oneself is secondary for all these teams of people.

Tennis was Don's show and his mistress. Tennis, his other love, cost him and his family dearly. No one could have demanded of him what he willingly gave, and it did not stop on the playing field. He never learned to set realistic boundaries to protect himself. He tried to please everyone. I asked myself what I could have done differently as his wife to help him live longer. I wish I had realized earlier and spared him more. Oh, yes, I could have listened to my mother's warning many years before: "You need to go to bed earlier. You'll never live long enough to pay off your mortgage," she had said.

My mother's warning had been prophetic. Don died before we paid off the mortgage. I made the last few payments on the home we had bought in 1958.

That is the way our lives were. I relived that last week and replayed my mental tapes. That too was part of grief.

CHAPTER VI

Prologue to the Trip

Minnie Scott, the president of Durham District United Methodist Church Women, had invited me to lunch with her at her home in Durham. We had become good friends as we served together in the volunteer organization. In the course of our time together, Minnie told me that Dr. Maxie Dunnam, then world editor of The Upper Room daily devotional, was hosting a tour to Oberammergau, Bavaria, in southern Germany. The idea of going interested me, and Don had agreed to the trip to Europe that was to start in Rome and include the Oberammergau Passion Play, an opportunity usually available only every ten years.

So it was that I had made the contact to request a berth for Don and me. On April 11, Don, home for lunch, answered the phone when Dr.Dunnam called to confirm our reservation for the trip. I was elated. Don's coaching responsibilities had him engaged when I went to the Holy Land and Rome in 1976 with a church group. Don had never been outside the United States.

I found myself fantasizing about how it would be for our June trip. While our parents lived, visiting his or mine at their homes constituted the only vacations we took. Several times after our sons were grown and out of the house, I accompanied Don on tennis trips to intercollegiate tennis championships in California,

Texas, and Georgia. I went with him and the team to Atlantic Coast Conference tennis matches in Virginia and Maryland. However, during those trips Don had many responsibilities. In thirty-three years, we had only one weekend vacation for just the two of us when we dove to Waltham, Mass., to attend his high-school reunion.

Someone else would be handling travel arrangements and reservations on this upcoming trip. We would be carefree. Without career demands and intrusions of the telephone, we could explore new places, new faces, and share experiences. I looked forward to having Don to myself for a little while.

We had not seen Beth since Poppa Skakle's death. I planned our agenda to include a few days to visit her at her home in Wareham, Mass., before we flew from Boston to Rome. After the tour with Maxie Dunnam ended in Zurich, Switzerland, we would continue, on our own, to meet Cliff in The Netherlands. Cliff, playing tennis in the Dutch Circuit, hoped to qualify for Wimbledon. We anticipated watching him play at both places.

After the tour, we would take a train from Zurich to Paris and do some sightseeing in Paris before joining Cliff in Tilburg. Finally, we would visit London. Don would see Wimbledon, the Mecca for tennis fans. My thrill would be to see our youngest son play there, a fulfillment of a dream for both Don and Cliff. This was our plan.

****

While the family surrounded me during those first days after Don's death, they encouraged me to go ahead with the trip. My brother Shanklin's widow, Ruby, agreed to accompany me. Ruby and I would follow the plan I had mapped out for Don and me. Don and I had not yet purchased our flight tickets, so Ruby planned to fly from Norfolk, Virginia. I would board my plane at Raleigh-Durham airport. She and I would meet in Boston. As far as the tour was concerned, all we needed to do was have Ruby's name substituted for Don's name. My assets, frozen due to Don's death, constituted one snag. Mona loaned me enough money to pay for my reservations. Ruby paid for hers, and our arrangements were easily completed.

Responsibilities related to my bereavement circumvented my plan to educate myself about the places we were to visit. My first priority was to send thank-you notes to those who had sent flowers, cards or brought gifts of food. Probate, once initiated, required my attention to ensure money would be released to repay Mona and provide spending money for the trip. I still had a job at Durham County General Hospital to fulfill.

I had been out of work for ten days following Don's death, when Mr. Stahl called and wanted to know if I was ready to come back to work. He explained that the policy of Durham County General called for only three days' leave. I may have read that at some point in my employment, but it had never affected me before. I had not even thought about work. I had enough vacation time to cover the extra week I had taken, but my absence affected the scheduling of the other pharmacists.

When I returned to work, Mr. Stahl called me into his office and kindly expressed his concern, which he had already done tangibly. One of the questions he asked was, "Do you think three days for bereavement leave is enough?"

I honestly did not know how to answer him. The question put me on the defensive. "I suppose so," I said.

A few days later, I stood checking medication carts, a daily responsibility of registered pharmacists in the pharmacy department of the hospital. Suddenly, I began to weep. Just then, Mr. Stahl walked past, saw my tears and distress and stopped to offer help.

I felt that I betrayed the stoic front I expected to maintain, and I was ashamed.

"I'm being bad." I said.

No, three days after an emotional loss is too little time. In our society of achievement and productivity, major surgery gives a more realistic sick leave than is provided for bereft employees. The loss of a close family member, in an emotional sense, is similar to major surgery.

After I went back to work, I found that the routine helped. I was grateful for my job. However, to perform well immediately after a major loss is like a bird trying to fly with one wing.

Even now, years since those first months of grief, I am unsure what a reasonable period-of-time for bereavement is. Perhaps it should be at least as long as the time—six weeks—given a new mother with her newborn baby.

I needed time to give the same tender, loving care to myself as I would to a baby and to have others help me. Everything was new in this world into which I had been thrust. In the "womb of marriage," Don had provided love, security, companionship, and safety. I felt overwhelmed by the expectations and routines that faced me as a widow. I needed time for my eyes to adjust to the light and to get my days and nights straight again.

I joined a spa to help relieve the stress I experienced as tingling sensations in my arms and to improve my health and self-image. The attendant measured my fat and my knees. It amused me when I learned my knees got fatter while I lost weight. I biked, swam, steamed, and exercised three or four times a week.

There is therapeutic value in work. It gave me value to be needed. Responsibility to others kept me getting up mornings. Mind discipline kept me from wandering aimlessly in the deep forests of regret: If only I...I should have...I could have...I wish I had. A schedule helped keep me focused on something other than my loss and misgivings. However, after an eight-hour shift and the walk to my car, I would dissolve into tears as I put the key into the ignition switch. The theme song of loneliness would resume and play as I drove home.

Pharmacist Sybil with pharmacists Bill Martin and Ben Bullock
at Durham County Hospital, 1985

I worked through May at the hospital. My trip was to begin June 5.
Fortunately, my vacation took me away from work for three more
weeks, time I needed to deal with the first days of grief.

CHAPTER VII

The Trip Begins

Andy and I were still writing thank-you notes until three in the morning of my flight day. We slept a few hours. Then I kept an appointment with my attorney, Chuck Beemer, later that morning. Chuck had prepared a lease for a lady to rent my business building at Hatteras. I needed to sign my will and planned to give my oldest son power of attorney over my financial affairs. By 11 o'clock that morning I had completed those chores. Energized by expectation, I rushed home from my lawyer's office to do last-minute packing and to plant and water flowers. Andy was not at home. I became anxious. I expected him to take me to the airport, and I needed to stop in Durham, eight miles away, to pick up my paycheck at the hospital and make a bank deposit. Andy showed up at 2 o'clock. As we drove toward the airport, I became nostalgic and philosophical, talking of life's eternal struggle to bring our feelings under the control of our minds and will. I talked. Andy listened. My intrepid words sounded false and flat to my own ears.

We were approaching Raleigh-Durham Airport when Andy said, "Mother, I'm proud of you. Do you think I should go to Europe?"

Cliff had already entered Andy into the Dutch Circuit Tennis event and arranged for Andy to join him in Amsterdam. Andy's question surprised me. Had he changed his mind? Would he go through with it? Would he show up in Europe?

Puzzled, I replied, "Andy, I want you to do what you want to do. Yes, I think the trip will be a very broadening experience for you."

As Piedmont flight 211 for Boston lifted off from Raleigh-Durham Airport at 4 PM, I remembered that Don should be next to me. Instead, my seat companions were a young woman, a biology major from Northwestern University, and a man in his forties returning to his wife and two daughters in Merrimac Valley, Massachusetts, from a business trip to Winston-Salem. Suddenly, sadness overwhelmed me.

Heavy traffic at the Boston airport delayed our landing. We circled, waiting for clearance, for many minutes. Ruby, who had arrived ahead, waited with Beth Skakle, Beth's daughter, Paula MacMillan, and Paula's son Bobby as I came into the waiting area.

My first trip to Boston with Don in 1946 had not been by plane. We had taken a Greyhound bus from Chapel Hill to Waltham, Massachusetts, to visit his parents at Christmas. I experienced the newness of New England and its people. It had snowed. Don wanted me to go ice-skating. Instead, I chose the warmth of watching TV with his parents at their Bacon-Street-home, while he went alone. Remembering, I regretted not having gone and tried to skate.

As Paula's husband Bob drove away from the airport, I saw road signs that reminded me of the places I visited with Don and his parents during that trip and others. By turning my attention to my companions, I managed to keep my tears from spilling over.

The next morning, Bob drove us to Beth's home in Wareham. Thoughts meandered through my mind that morning as we drove along, and I remembered another ride when Don had been with me. When had that been? We had followed this same route. How would this visit with Beth be without Don here?

As never before, I considered the pain and loss Ruby had

felt when Shanklin died in January 1976. Three widows—Beth, Ruby, and me! Would we be able to comfort one another? Would I find new answers or revelations? Would Don travel with Andy and Cliff as part of the "cloud of witnesses" that surrounds us like God's presence? Would this trip help my sons and me face our futures without their father?

We arrived at Wareham around 11 o'clock the morning of June 6. After coffee—tea for Bob—Bob left to return to Hudson. Beth, Ruby, and I went farther down The Cape to have lunch at The Dolphin. Then Beth drove us down to the canal to take a brief walk. I found it hard to be interested or appreciative. I noted the red sails as they passed. There had been a song—"Red Sails in the Sunset." I'd never seen red sails before. The brisk wind chilled me, and I longed for bodily comfort.

After Ruby had gone to bed that night, Beth and I talked. I valued her counsel and wisdom. Self-determination under God's guidance seemed a fine goal. "However, after I went to bed I felt guilty. I knew that the anger I felt toward Don for having died and left me alone was unreasonable. He had been gone less than two months. My thoughts were conflicting and troublesome. In my mind, I went from idolizing him to deriding him. I felt deserted and betrayed. Had I revealed too much of my anger to Beth? Did she understand? Finally, I slept, having acknowledged my inability to control life, which holds both the helpful and the hurtful."

I wrote in my journal-

> *I will be glad to have traveled through the barren fields and to arrive at the verdant, lush shaded areas of rest and peace. The ground between does not seem far. My traveling companion is Jesus ,and he gives Ruby and Beth to me to guide me over unfamiliar ground.*

June 7 dawned: Mona and Virgil's wedding anniversary. There would be no celebration for them. A breach in their marriage contract made divorce imminent. More pain, involving people I love.

Ruby, Beth, and I left the house to shop at Kay Windsor's outlet in a nearby town. I bought a couple of dresses. We had lunch at a Woolworth's store.

That evening we talked about our early lives. A psychiatrist I talked to the evening before my departure said: "Remembering the bitter prepares for the sweet." I remembered so much bitter. "I'm just being honest!" I said in my defense. Yet those honest utterances made me feel ugly.

Ruby and I were happy to attend St. Patrick's in Wareham with Beth on Sunday morning. To be in church on Sunday is to be "at home" for a Christian. The priest spoke of bread. Ruby commented: "The three of us—Catholic, United Methodist, and Assembly of God—are one in Christ, though we eat different bread."

We enjoyed a simple lunch after church. We went to Quintals at Buzzard Bay for dinner, where I had been with Poppa, Beth, and Don when Don and I had driven to Maine in the new Buick he had purchased. We went to help celebrate Poppa Skakle's eightieth birthday in 1976 with Caroline and Gordon in Stockton Springs. We had driven back to Wareham and spent a couple of days with Poppa and Beth there before driving home. That's when we had driven that route to Wareham that I had remembered earlier! My emotions flooded my heart so that the barriers of my mind could hardly hold back the sobs that rose in my throat.

On the morning we were to leave, Beth drove us to The Wayside Inn in Sudbury for a lovely lunch. Twenty-four years before, Don, toddler Eddie, and I had visited this place with Mom Skakle, who had died in 1968. It seemed such a short time ago. Memories and tears intermingled as I tried to control my thoughts so I would not fill my plate with tears.

After lunch, Beth drove back to the MacMillan's at Hudson, and Bob drove us to the airport for our 8 o'clock flight. Beth went with us to say good-bye.

The flight to Rome would take seven hours. Music over the earphones on the plane, made me cry. The music of my life was

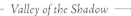
silenced and dancers no longer danced. Grief shrouded the beauty I saw and the beauty I heard. Grief colors everything gray. I dislike gray, except for painting porches.

CHAPTER VIII

Rome to Venice

Ruby and I arrived in Rome in early morning. I felt nervous and insecure as I managed to call Cliff on the public telephone. That effort, the strangeness of the country and unfamiliar surroundings made me feel like an alien on Earth. After an hour and a half wait, I learned why our tour group had not arrived. I discovered that they had missed their flight in New York and should arrive on an Italian flight at 3:30 PM.

With the help of a stranger, I ordered bitter coffee with ham on a dry bun that looked like a hot-dog roll for Ruby and me. Three-thirty arrived and passed. It was 5 PM before I finally greeted our group as they arrived. While I ran interference and made inquiries, Ruby watched our luggage, the role she chose then and later.

I rejoiced as I followed the others from the airport. It was good to be following someone who knew what to expect and was taking us where we should go. Finally, our tour had begun! On our way to Hotel Palentino, we saw something of Rome—something besides the inside of the airport! From the windows of the bus I watched the cars darting about and realized how different the pattern of traffic is from ours in the USA.

It had been a very long time since those dry sandwiches and bitter coffee. After settling in our hotel room, our dinner seemed the more delicious for its contrast to our first fare. We were to have some form of spaghetti every meal in Rome, either as an entrée or only as an appetizer. Also, every meal included hard rolls with air in the middle. I wondered if they had a special name.

The tour the next morning began at nine. Ruby and I were up at seven to have rolls, jelly, and the thick Italiano cafe. I cut mine with milk. Our table companions were a couple of girls from Lexington, Kentucky. During that first day, we visited Rome's main square and Corso, Rome's longest street. We saw the ruins of two ancient pagan temples on our way to the Pantheon. At the Vatican we enjoyed seeing the Sistine Chapel, and I bought a broach or two from a vendor. We saw less statuary than when I visited Rome in 1976, on the way home from the Holy Land. I was disappointed for the others in the group, and for me, that we did not see Michelangelo's Moses.

At an outdoor garden restaurant off the Appian Way, we enjoyed a very pleasant lunch. Arbors were covered with what looked to me to be Virginia creeper, something we try to eliminate from our gardens. Handsome young men in white shirts and black britches served us. Members of another tour group put sunglasses on the bust of a noble Roman citizen, situated to the right of our table, and took pictures of themselves. They amused us with their antics.

The ability to take pleasure in this lunch interlude seemed paradoxical. Should I enjoy this? Anything?

After lunch, the bus took us along the Appian Way to the Catacombs. Nothing I knew prepared me for what they are—places where the dead were buried. The Catacombs are important to Christians because they were a place of refuge for our early brothers and sisters during persecution. Maxie Dunnam, author of *Alive in Christ* (Abington Press, copyright 1982), had us remember that others alive in Christ sought this place of the dead to stay alive and maintain their faith during days of persecution of the early church. He had saved bread and wine from our lunch. With them, he served communion to all of us in a little chapel in the Catacombs. He prayed for "our living loved and our dead loves." Did he have me in mind? Did he know how that phrase struck me with longing? Of course, others had lost dear ones. I reminded myself that I was not the only one.

The next day, June 12, we traveled by bus down Palatino Hill, passing Celus Hill. We left the old west gate of the ancient city, having stopped a short while near the ruins of The Forum. Outside the city walls, we traveled pleasant tree-lined avenues, past Circus Maximus, until we came to the beautiful Basilica of St. Paul Outside the Walls, built over St. Paul's tomb and restored after a fire in the last century. St. Paul Outside the Walls had been one of my favorite sights on my first trip to Rome. I had forgotten how large and beautiful it is. Compared to St. Peter's, it is quite small. However, St. Paul Outside the Walls is made up of many chapels. In one of them, a Catholic priest was giving mass, and I was moved to pray. I knelt there with my heart broken and my spirit needing to be healed. I remembered St. Paul's devotion and his sacrifices for Christ. I asked God to help me be yielded.

The Borghese Museum, filled with statues of the splendid bodies of Roman athletes, made me acutely aware of my loss of the physical body of the man I loved.

Oh, Jesus my Lord, you must show me the way through the unbroken days that stretch ahead without Don. I cannot walk them without your help.

How am I to live cut in two, with one-part ashes in an urn in Chapel Hill? Show me, please, Oh, God!

After lunch and a nap, Ruby and I went alone to Trivi Fountain. We walked from there to the Spanish Steps, a colorful gathering place for artists and peddlers of leather and beads. One was selling a peculiar little pear-shaped instrument on which he played Beethoven's "Ode to Joy." Beyond the Steps area, we visited an old church and bought a chocolate ice cream cone, a rarity on our tour. We decided not to go to Trivoli Gardens with the group later.

Andy's call from London that evening took me by surprise. He had made it! On the same side of the ocean, he was still far from me. I worried about him, traveling alone. Cliff had traveled abroad before, so I did not worry about him. This was Andy's first trip. I sought to relax, to trust God for Andy and to trust Andy to be able to handle anything that might happen to him.

June 13, we left Rome on a sunny day. The roads were good. Maxie gave a devotion and his wife, Jerri, led us in a couple of songs as we traveled over the hills and through the valleys. Yellow, lavender, and red wildflowers were visible from the bus windows. I recognized oleander bushes, not yet in bloom. Oleander grows well on Hatteras Island, where I was born, though I do not believe it is native to the island.

As we traveled north, the terrain became more mountainous. Orchards dotted hillsides. In the agricultural area where we were driving, the bundles in the fields gave witness of the harvest. Grapevines were plentiful along the route. Stucco houses were orange-brown, pink, or mustard-yellow with orange tile roofs. The water in the rivers seemed as green as the foliage and trees. Perhaps the water reflected those colors.

As we approached Assisi, we passed nicer homes. Construction seemed to consist of concrete beams as foundation for all levels. The light brick they used looked almost pink.

We met Father George, a fat little man in a black habit, as we began our tour in Assisi. He was to be our guide and told us that he came from Connecticut. A human trying to become like St. Francis, his humor seemed to border on irreverence. However, when he witnessed to how he felt about obedience to Christ, my doubts were allayed. He led us through the very beautiful Church of the Angels.

At the St. Clare Altar in Assisi, a prayer, by St Francis before the Crucifix, caught my attention:

> All highest, glorious God, cast your light into the
> darkness of my heart.

Give me right faith, firm hope, perfect charity—
and profound humility,
With wisdom and perception, O Lord, so that I may do
what is truly your holy will.—Amen

I knelt at the altar below the plaque and claimed the prayer for my own, remembering what Father George had told us of the devotion of St. Clare and St. Francis to God. I needed God's help to do his holy will.

Father George's observation when we approached the golden altar changed my perspective forever. I cannot quote him. In essence, he said that all the beauty spent to glorify God is of little worth in relation to God himself and the beauty of heaven. Awe and understanding came to me as Father George pointed to the altar made of gold and said: "All the gold belongs to God, after all!"

All things are God's. Why do we try to withhold anything from Him? Who has more claim to the beauty and riches of Earth than does God Almighty? Don belonged to God and "all that dwell therein." Yet, I would argue with God about that weeks later.

Our arrival outside Florence, Italy, came a short time later. A statue of Michelangelo's David, not the most famous one, stood on an elevated place overlooking the city. From this vantage point we had a spectacular view of the city. Dr. Dunnam had earlier spoken of the need for Protestants to appreciate the Catholics preservation of art for all of us. I began to understand the significance of that statement as we stood looking over the lovely city of Florence. We toured Florence, riding on the bus, and saw the outside of several more cathedrals on our way to the Monginevro Hotel, a modern hotel with smaller rooms than those of the older hotels.

On June 14, our mustachioed guide, who wore glasses and had curly shoulder-length hair, looked like an art object, in his white leather pants, a shirt with blue and green horizontal stripes, and white loafers. He took us to Acadamie de Arts to see Michelangelo's David—the real one! I'll leave the description to an artist, but as

I looked at that white marble David I thought of another young, beautiful athlete, whom I had loved and married in 1947. My reaction was both physical and emotional.

The Cathedral de Fiore—the most beautiful of all—is built of green, white, and rose marble. Its colors signify hope, charity, and faith. The baptistery, dedicated to John the Baptist, stands next to the cathedral and has a golden door, called the Gate of Paradise.

After seeing that, we visited the Medici Chapels and the New Sacristy, which Michelangelo built before he did the Last Judgment of Sistine Chapel. Next, on to Piazza Signoria, a colorful place in front of Loggia Della Signoria, with statues by Michelangelo as well as other sculptors. I hated that the pigeons had defaced the statues.

That afternoon, when Ruby and I rested, I slept and dreamed of Don. I heard his voice. He smiled at me and kissed me as he had done all those years to affirm me and declare his love. It was only when life pressed hard and responsibility caused stress that his impatience surfaced. I awoke in tears.

I waited for a phone call that will never come and remembered the person I wanted to call could not call. Life is made up of dreaming and waking.

As I walked later that day, I found myself thinking I had been fortunate to have a good man's love—to have known what it is to love someone as deeply and totally as I loved Don. As a mortal, I loved my memories, and I remembered that Poppa Skakle said after Mom's death, "I can't live on memories."

I did not feel that I could either. For love not shared cannot be love. Love that has no direction toward another is grief. Those bereaved by estrangement and divorce must know what I felt. Their circumstances must cause worse frustration, when they are torn between hope and despair continually. I thought of Mona and of Andy!

Sometimes I feel anesthetized to the point that, while I know the pain is there, I am unable to feel it. I am afraid to feel it. I trust that it is you, Lord, understanding human grief, interceding with the Father, and protecting me until I can bear it. I'm glad for the tears. Tears should be shed when something as sweet as our love has ceased to be— tears of sadness, tears of joy, tears of quiet thankfulness. Please, Lord, protect my heart from anguished bitter tears—from frustration. Keep me in your peace and enable me to glorify you in every moment of being. Amen

On June 15, we passed over a beautiful mountain range on our way to Venice. Maxie led a worship service as we rode along on the bus and asked for prayer concerns. Raveena, our destination, was our only stop along the way. Our purpose was to view one or two of the many sixth-century tombs. The music of a wedding in progress in the fortress like brick church adjacent to the gravesites caused me to weep. There were many elegant mosaics to see through bleary eyes.

At lunch at The Laughing Rooster, Bill and June Beeler sat at our table. In his opening conversation, Bill, a tennis buff, asked about Cliff's tennis. Then he offered to provide information regarding investments. I feel he did not mean to upset me and I do not understand why his offering to give me financial advice caused my reaction. However, the sudden reminder of Don's death two months earlier made me fight tears. The others at the table were probably embarrassed too. It was a bad moment for both Bill and me.

Yes, there were decisions and adjustments that I would need to make when I returned home. I definitely did not intend to make investments with Bill Beeler. Although his intentions were probably well meant, his timing was very poor. I felt suspicious and affronted by his suggestion that I make investments with him. Someone at home in Chapel Hill would help me invest Don's insurance money.

Marty McNary, one of the young people in our group, entertained us with song during the ride afterward. His performance contrasted greatly to the moment at lunch. The attention was on Marty instead of on me. His lyrics and compositions delighted our ears.

As we approached Venice, the land became lower and almost marshy. At about four o'clock, we arrived at a point where we had to transfer from the bus to a motor launch. The launch took us to Grand Hotel Luna, the prettiest, most elegant hotel we had yet seen.

We put our luggage in our room and went to see St. Mark's Cathedral in St. Mark Square, with its many pigeons. Inside the cathedral were many beautiful golden mosaics. Afterward, Ruby and I sat outside to rest in the sunshine awhile before going over the water, by footbridge, to the glass factory. There we bought glass Italian beads. On our way back to the hotel, Ruby found a beautiful lace tablecloth, and I bought an embroidered blouse and a brown leather handbag. We made our purchases under the pressure of time—we were rushing to arrive back at the hotel in time for dinner. We just made it.

After dinner, Ruby declined the planned gondola trip. And, she discovered we had no hot water. Therefore, I stopped at the desk on my way to the gondolas to tell them our room needed hot water. I then took a position in the front of one of the seven gondolas. We began to move smoothly through the water. A gondolier, other than the one at the oar in mine, began to sing a love song to the accompaniment of accordion music. Suddenly, tears came without warning. Without a handkerchief, trying to hide my tears, I let them run down my face and into the water of the canals to become a part of the Adriatic Sea. Nothing, not any place, can be more romantic than Venice.

Oh, honey! I want you here so much. This would have been a great day for us. It is Father's Day, and probably our sons are very sad today. However, their sadness is not as mine. They have not had grief as this before. But the music of their lives has not been silenced. Andy may feel similar grief because he and Bonnie are separated. You were my music. We danced to the same rhythm because we loved one another. Maybe Andy felt like that about Bonnie. Maybe not. He has more to cope with than I do. He's so young and vulnerable to lose a grandfather, a wife, and a father in less than a year—and to be fired from his position as tennis professional at Kinston Country Club.

Life teaches us to be emotionally tough or to perish. Either we learn to swim or we drown in our tears.

You taught me a lot about fighting the good fight. Sometimes I thought we were not dancing to the same music. However, maybe we were, more than we knew. I suspect we were like two generals with the same objective but who failed to coordinate their efforts. No wonder we kept shooting the ally instead of the enemy. But we did learn more about strategy and communication at the end.

When we returned from the gondola ride and I went to our room, I found Ruby near hysteria. When I entered the room, she said, "Sybil, I'm glad you're back. The most awful thing happened right after you left."

"What happened, Ruby?"

She started to tell me her story. "I had taken off my clothes to take a bath and was looking at my lace tablecloth. I heard someone at the door. I yelled, 'Don't you come in here!' while wrapping the lace tablecloth around me. But he wouldn't stop. I rushed to the door and slammed it shut and bolted it."

I doubled up with laughter, and she stood there dumbfounded. "Oh, Ruby, it had to be the man who came to see about the hot water," I said.

Ruby did not laugh. "It is not funny!" she said peevishly. "I was so scared: I didn't want to take a bath. I thought I was going to be raped!"

CHAPTER IX

Venice to Lucerne

Vendors swarmed like hungry mosquitoes upon our group when we arrived by launch from Venice to the dry ground where our travel bus awaited us on June 16. We took a brief look at their wares before entering the bus to begin our journey to Vienna, Austria.

Soon our bus began to climb. Distant mountains became mountains surrounding us. Maxie led us in praising God as we rode along. The streams like aquamarine ribbon ran through the valley against the gray earth. The various green hues of the evergreen and hardwood trees covered the mountainsides, while the bridges and tunnels breaching the ravines added interest to the terrain.

We had gone only a short distance before one couple discovered they had forgotten to pick up their passports at the hotel desk in Venice. At the Austrian border stop, they left us to return by train to retrieve their passports at Hotel Luna.

Snow-capped mountains seemed closer. As we entered Austria, we stopped to exchange our money—lire to schillings. My spirit lifted as we moved upward. My excitement and anticipation surprised me. I thanked God for my durable spirit and the new hope I felt like a silent song of praise and adoration. I felt full of happy anticipation.

We stopped for lunch at Klagenfurt, Austria, a name with significance for me because Cliff, traveling with Tennis Europe in 1973 or 1974, played a tennis tournament in Klagenfurt that resulted in a $100-dollar phone call home—a considerable sum for the Skakle family. We had given him permission to call us if he should have a good win, and he did, at Klagenfurt! I had an egg for lunch, my first since leaving home, which tasted so good! The beef lung soup, a new fare for me, was quite tasty too. Two meats, salad, three vegetables, and dessert made a virtual feast. Eating such food, I realized how tired I had become of Italian pasta. American-Italian sauces are richer and better than any we ate in Italy.

As we left Klagenfurt, the countryside became more and more mountainous, for we were in the Alps. Homes were still of stucco and brick, but the roofs were slate instead of terra cotta. Wooden balconies made them look, as we expected, like Austrian chalets.

I had been reading Don Gosset's book, *You Get What You Say*, and finished it that day. His caution to readers to speak the positive made sense to me, for it paralleled the Scripture, which tells us: "pray believing you receive." I wrote in my journal of my intent to use God's power and promises to speak thereafter from faith and hope in Christ Jesus. I determined that my prayers would change from anxiety-based requests forevermore. I confess that I did not always live up to my vow of faith and hope during the next two years. But on that day, I felt invincible!

The crush of the tourist crowds in Vienna made us wish we had started sightseeing earlier. Our first stop was the Belvedere Palace. I think it was there that the gleaming, round -sided stoves, decorated like fine china art objects, intrigued me. I wondered if they had been as functional as those brown enameled ones of my childhood.

The Belvedere Palace, so named because of its location for a view of the city, is huge. (Belvedere in Italian literally means "beautiful view.") Eugene of Savoy purchased the land in 1697. He kept one architect busy from 1714 to 1721 designing and building the four stages of the magnificent Austrian Baroque palaces. The

Lower Belvedere was built first. Workers completed the luxurious Upper Belvedere, started in 1720, in 1721. Belvedere sustained damage during World War II.

The gardens between the Upper Belvedere and the Lower Belvedere consist of green hedges that seemed to stretch for what might have been several city blocks. As we began to walk on the wide paths, I looked down at my sturdy brown oxfords and was thankful I had purchased them before leaving home.

There were other palaces we might have explored, the Imperial and Schonbrun. Austria is an old empire, and Vienna is a very huge city. We could not possibly see it all in one morning. We had a tiny taste to whet our appetites.

I know little of European history. Travel broadens a person, but to better enjoy what one sees, one needs to know a little about what is being explored. Imagine playing Scrabble without being able to read or spell. That is sort of the way I felt that morning. Dumb!

After a delicious Austrian lunch, Ruby and I, along with fellow traveler Hilda Lemaster, rode the public transportation system to visit a shopping area. Ruby and I were seated in the conveyance with a Japanese couple, who were visiting an Austrian woman. The attractive Austrian woman chattered as if I understood every word she spoke. The Japanese couple had to act as our interpreter, explaining to me what she said and to her what I said. It did not slow her down one bit. She continued to chatter and smiled brightly when we parted, as though we were bosom buddies.

The stores in the business district did not overly impress me, maybe because I dislike shopping. Ruby made the purchase for which we came and we began to think about getting back to the hotel. We had plans for the evening. How were we going to get back? None of us had a clue. It seemed safe for me to stop two men in business suits to ask for directions. They were kind. Being ignorant travelers that we were, we depended on the patience and mercy of those we approached in the countries we visited. Finally, on public transportation again, a matron in a red blouse, who spoke no English but understood body language and our visible bewilderment, indicated to us where we should disembark. We had arrived safe and sound.

After an early supper, another traveling companion joined the original three adventurers to go to a concert. The lovely weather, the beautiful music, and lighthearted people encouraged me. However, the lovely, familiar waltzes the orchestra played following the main concert undid me. I watched the people below our balcony and nearest the orchestra, while the Danube River flowed nearby and strains of the "Blue Danube Waltz" filled the evening air. I longed to be dancing in Don's arms .My feelings seemed like self-pity. So, I practiced Gosset's positive approach, turned my thoughts to God, and redirected my attention to my companions.

June 17 journal entry: *Don, I want to talk to you as I do to God. Is it right that I should? I know that I must live my life without you. I mean to be a credit to you and, in obedience to God, to live out my life to its very end. I mean, with the help of Our Precious Lord, to go on without you in joy, praise, and singing.*

This seemed brave and possible. I did not recognize my lapses into euphoria as denial. I had heard that denial is one of the first phases of grief, but when I would begin to feel full of hope and somewhat happy, I thought I was making progress. Perhaps it might represent a small step forward. I did not recognize it as denial. If someone had identified my mood swings as denial, I would have taken issue with it.

I did not expect to hear from Cliff before we reached Munich. He called that evening after we returned from the concert, before I made my intended call to him. I was happy to hear that Andy had arrived. Bad news was that robbers relieved him of two hundred dollars in Amsterdam his first night in Europe. Poor Andy!

June 18 I had a troubled dream, amounting to a nightmare, and I awoke full of tears. I asked God for protection as I fought the doubt that Don did not love me; and the fear that he had betrayed me. Perhaps my psychiatrist could help me understand my insecurities; when I returned home, I would share it with him.

As soon as we arrived at Holiday Inn Munich, Leopoldstrasse, I phoned Cliff. His fiancee, Mary, and he came by car while we were eating supper. Cliff drove Kevin Dunnam, Ruby, and me to meet the others at the Platz Hofhaus, where we sat around tables to enjoy a lively program of music and dancing. The waiters served the whole assemblage glasses of beer, which seemed to come with the territory, the cover charge, I suppose. Cliff drank mine, but I don't remember who drank Ruby's.

Since Cliff and Mary had not eaten, Ruby and I went with them to a nearby restaurant. When we started back to the motel afterward, Cliff got lost. It was 11:30 PM before we found our way back. Ruby went up to the room and left Cliff, Mary, and me to talk.

Resentment and anger defined Cliff's grief. He was angry that his dad had worked so hard and his salary had been so low. He talked and shed tears, while I put on a happy face, thinking my being brave would help him. He should be reassured if I were okay, I thought. I really believed I spoke truthfully when I claimed that I was doing well. Surrounded by wonderful, caring people ,and fully engaged day by day, I received emotional support, especially from Ruby. I do not know how much my mood and well-being can be attributed to my companions.

June 19 we were on our way to Oberammergau, in the Bavarian area of Germany. As we began that leg of our trip and tour of Munich, our bus driver made a detour to Glockenspiel— the town hall. At 11 AM, we were to see life size-figures of a man and woman come out of the tower on top of the building. Like a giant cuckoo clock, when the music began, the figures came out of the tower and took a dance turn or two before returning to the depths of the tower.

The onionlike dome of the cloister, Ettall, which is the tallest landmark of the village, caught my eye as we arrived in Oberammergau. We were in time for family-style lunch at a small local restaurant.

Our host family, Alois and Luise Macherpocher, received Ruby and me and helped us get settled. We were delighted with our bedroom and the soft, white down comforters, which immediately invited Ruby to take a nap.

We awoke on the morning of June 20 to a rainy, chilly day. Our hosts provided a substantial breakfast to prepare us for a day at the theater. Our coffee that morning was delicious—the best we had had in Europe. The clean, neat surroundings of the Macherpocher home were pleasant.

Many residents of the town make their living carving wooden objects, while others, like our householders, take care of the thousands of tourists who come to see the Passion Play. The play, first performed in 1634, portrays the suffering and death of Jesus. The all-day presentation consists of two segments: one before lunch and one afterward—in the afternoon. In the performance we witnessed, I felt the parts of Peter and John were weak, and the man who played Judas, too old. But the older man had talent, and his part seemed the strongest of all, which I found disconcerting. The protagonist's role in a story is to show the strength of the main character. I felt this Judas overshadowed Jesus. Sometimes in life, the bad seems to overshadow the good. Perhaps it was done that way on purpose. Artists have their reasons that we are not to question, or so a friend of mine told me. So, elephants with purple polka dots are okay.

During the Black Plague, the people of the town made a vow to perform the play every ten years in gratitude for the end of the dreadful pestilence. The present generation continues to honor the vow made by their ancestors, and the villagers fill all the roles of the play. An extra showing given in 1984 commemorated the end of the plague 250 years before.

Bundled up in rain gear, we tried to keep warm, while we sat on wooden benches under covered wooden outdoor stands. Would Don have enjoyed this? Certainly, I would have been doubly blessed to have shared this and the other experiences with him. As I looked over the crowd, made up of older people for the most part, I wondered if Ruby and I looked as old as they did. And it rained and rained and rained.

We left early the next morning, after our householder provided breakfast. Johnnie, our driver, resumed his responsibilities, and we rode through other beautiful mountains on our way to Lucerne, Switzerland. Flowers in Oberammergau and along the way were mostly familiar ones: peonies, green- and red-leafed begonias, purple ageratum, and yellow marigold. The flowers and another anxious dream that morning made me long for home. I wondered about my flowers and the dogs, Suki and Nikki. I wondered how being back at home alone, with nothing to anticipate, would feel. I wanted some guarantee that life would be bearable. I kept yielding, insofar as I could. I knew my peace depended on being patient. I could not hurry grief. I must learn to wait for God's answers and for time to pass.

When we arrived in Lucerne, Switzerland, our nice room had bed comforters with zebra-like print. The carpet was brown and beige. A mahogany desk, chairs, and coffee table completed the décor. Our spacious bathroom and the piped-in music were pleasing, and Ruby and I expressed to one another our appreciation for the richness of our surroundings. Double glass doors, from ceiling to floor, provided a view of the broad walk and lovely Lake Lucerne beside it.

Kim and Kerry, daughters of Maxie and Jerri Dunnam, and their friend, Kathy, met us at Lucerne. Many young people were traveling in Europe that summer. I admired their spunk and thought Ruby and I should be able to manage if they could. I never would have been so brave when I was their age. After dinner, several of our group assembled in the lobby with the girls to hear of their travel experiences.

By now, everyone in our group knew I was newly bereaved. Bessie B. slipped her arm around my shoulder as we started up to our rooms. "Sybil, you should do as much as you can for others. It will help you."

Certainly, I knew I would need to find outlets for my love and spend that love for others. I did not suppose I would be able to support an Indian girl as Bessie said she did. For now, I felt so needy that I doubted my ability to do much for anyone else. My church family would be supportive. I did not believe anything or anyone capable of filling the void in my life—not ever!

Being single again, I had a great curiosity about how other single women felt about their singleness. Ruby had been where I was when she lost my brother. Now she had a special someone in her life, and I expected her to marry within the year. By the time our trip ended, she would know her heart and make a decision. At supper I asked one of the younger women at our table how she felt about her singleness.

"I like my freedom. I would not want to give it up to fix meals and take care of the needs of another person," she said.

Funny, I never thought of chores as a sacrifice of freedom. They were tradeoffs for the things Don did for the family and for me. I could not say that I liked to cook, while I had a friend, Nancy, who said she cooked to relax after her work as a department supervisor. Cooking is not on my like-to-do list. As a wife and mother, I sought to prepare balanced, healthy meals. To cut costs in other ways, I did my own hair, except for haircuts; gave my own permanents; and cut the boys' hair. Even though I did not work outside the home while our sons were young, I believed I carried my share of the financial burden by careful management of Don's income. I washed, ironed, patched, cleaned, sewed, and paid the bills with the money Don made. When we were first married, he wrote the checks, but it soon fell to me to do it. I can't remember our even discussing it. I like working with figures and am a good manager of home and money.

Don kept the lawn and earned the money, which I spent for the food I cooked. Don's university salary provided for little more than the necessities for our family of five. I did not work at pharmacy, except for a few relief jobs, when the boys were young. I stayed home to run interference. Don and I liked that I could. He did not want me to work outside the home. Like his father, he expected to be the bread winner of the family and wanted his sons to have their mother at home. I liked having Don come home for lunch. I liked his company. I appreciated being available to support our sons in their athletic pursuits. I liked our life. I liked marriage and motherhood—most of the time!

On Sunday morning, June 22, after breakfast, Ingram Parmley, an Episcopal priest, presented communion and led a worship service for our travel group in the lobby of the hotel. During his discourse, he remarked that our trip together had made him appreciate anew the different expressions of faith. "The Eastern Orthodox emphasize the Incarnation and have the best Christmas celebration; Catholics concentrate on the Crucifixion and the suffering Christ bore for us; Protestants celebrate Easter as our great high point and, probably, black Southern Baptists do it best of all."

Our time together was almost over. In the part of the service called "passing the peace," we expressed our gratitude for the friendships fostered during our days together. We felt sad as we anticipated our goodbyes the next morning.

After the service, several of us put on our walking shoes for a trip downtown to see the famous "Lion of Lucerne," a huge lion carved in solid rock. It is a memorial for the Swiss Guards who died defending King Louis XVI at Tuileries, the royal palace on the right bank of the river Seine in Paris, in 1792 during the French Revolution.

After we had looked at the stately beast, Ruby and I went to see the Glacier Gardens nearby. Mayme Seeders and Hilda Lemaster, our companions, left us to return to the hotel, and we followed soon afterward to get ready for a planned tour, which would include a full afternoon of activity.

After lunch, we put on warmer clothing, suggested for our trip to Mount Pilatus. The trip began with a bus ride. We then transferred to cable cars, which held four people each. Those took us to an elevation of 4,326 feet before we transferred to larger cable cars, which ascended to 7,000 feet. There, on top of Mount

Pilatus, we found snow as high as our heads. We took pictures against the snow bank and saw our breath against the thirty-five-degree air. We saw smaller hotels as we rode up the heights, and the ski resort hotel on top of the mountain had a restaurant, where we were able to have light refreshment.

Coming down off the mountain, we sat straight in the red compartments. The seats on the train angled at about 48 degrees. From the windows of the tram, we saw a couple carrying milk cans, going home. I attempted to photograph the lovely purple wildflowers on the bank near their home.

Reaching the bottom of the mountain, forty-eight of us transferred to a motor launch. Forty-three were members of our tour group; Maxie's daughters and friend; Madalyn, our attractive tour guide; and the captain made up the group. The sun was warm. The twenty-four-mile ride, which took about an hour and a half, was pleasant. Madalyn described points of interest along the shore. We enjoyed watching water skiers, propelled by the winds in their sails. Madalyn told us that the water temperature was only sixteen degrees. Our final day—from worship in the morning at the hotel to those final moments on Lake Lucerne—seemed perfect.

On Monday morning, June 23, we left early for Zurich, the largest and probably the richest city of Switzerland. As we rode along, Madalyn gave us information that helped us understand more about this beautiful county. In Switzerland, they voted down socialized medicine because it would be too costly. Instead, they had compulsory medical insurance in the twenty-six cantons of the country. Another startling thing she told us is that every man between twenty and thirty-two years of age is part of the militia. Each man keeps his gun, ammunition, and uniform at home. If he should be called, he can respond at a moment's notice. Because Switzerland is too small to fight, its government finds it wise to remain neutral, but there is a plan to protect the country should necessity dictate. Switzerland was the richest country in the world in 1980 and probably still is.

CHAPTER X

On Our Own in Paris

Ruby and I said goodbye to our traveling companions in Zurich. We walked around the train station, had breakfast and I bought a newspaper, the first I had seen in weeks. The news was not good, but was certainly noteworthy with more inflation, the economic summit talks, June 22-23 in Venice. The editor considered the talks futile, as they were complicated by OPEC nations and by Soviet's rule in Afghanistan. At least our cups of coffee were good.

We checked our baggage and I bought our reservations during the morning. After lunch, Ruby and I hit most of the stores along the main street, looking more than buying. We had lots of time to kill, since our train to Paris did not leave until that evening.

We had been great friends since Ruby came into the family when I was only fifteen years old. She was six years older, married to my only brother. We had never talked about a misunderstanding that had alienated my brother and me before he died. I needed to tell her my side of the story. While we drank a leisurely cup of coffee near the end of the day, I had chance to do that and. I was grateful for that opportunity.

When I made our reservations for the train ride that morning, I had trouble with communication across the language barrier. My two years of high school French did not help me one bit. I thought

I made reservations for cushioned seats on the second level of the train. When we got on the train, we learned we were going to sleep in middle bunks and there were six in each compartment. The real shock came when the conductor came, fifteen minutes out of Zurich, to collect tickets that we did not have.

A young American woman who knew French helped the conductor and me communicate with one another. No, he would not take a Travelers Checks for the three hundred and thirty French francs we owed for our tickets. Surely they would not leave two, dumb widow women along the train tracks in Basal? Then I remembered. We wanted a cup of coffee. We went into a bank and I cashed a Traveler Check for one hundred dollars and converted ninety-five of it into French francs. I had enough to pay the conductor for both our fares and enough for our breakfast in Paris the next morning. Barely! Our guardian angels had taken care of us.

The conductor seemed amused by my discomfort and told the interpreter to tell me that he would be coming back for the rest of his money. I kept expecting him to come back. I still wonder if we got a free ride from Zurich to Basal

A young couple had the top bunks. A middle-aged Swiss couple would occupy the lower ones. Our bunks, Ruby's and mine, were the middle ones on either side of the compartment. The Swiss woman helped us, probably in self-defense, to make up our bunks. It was late and time for all of us to be in bed. Finally, I managed to sleep.

When I awoke on June 24, my first thought was of Andy. It was his twenty-eighth birthday. The train pulled into *Gore de L'est* around 7 a.m. I called the *Hotel du Lion d'Or*, (Hotel of the Golden Lion) where Cliff said he made reservations for us. The person, who did not speak English, managed to say, "Call back at nine."

Ruby and I had our continental breakfast. Then I stood in line, behind two young American women--from Miami and California--to get French currency in exchange for our Travelers Checks. Afterward, at information, I paid a young woman six francs to call the hotel for me again. Obtaining directions was vexing. After we found the baggage room, we loaded our bags onto a cart and Ruby volunteered to watch them while I went to see about our tickets for Amsterdam. I would gladly have traded places with her. I knew no more about traveling in Europe than she did, but I did what I had to do. I solved the mystery of ticket buying with the help of a young woman from Detroit, Michigan. We waited at least fifteen minutes before Ruby and I found a taxi. By the time, we arrived at the hotel it was 11:30 AM. We had spent our first Paris morning in the train station.

The hotel doorway opened off a narrow one-way street. The door, trimmed in brass, accounted for "golden" in its name and was the hotel's only claim to elegance. The entranceway, as wide as the door, had a stair ascending to the left. Worn red-carpeted steps led upward. A young man came down the steps and relieved Ruby and me of our train cases, leaving us to struggle with the large heavier bags and hand luggage. We learned from his English-speaking wife that he was Spanish. A clerk at the reception desk, to the right of the stairs and at right angles with the stair opening, could not find a record of Cliff's deposit. Therefore, I paid ninety francs to register us at hotel. A young cleaning- woman came forward to help us up another flight of uneven, worn red-carpeted stairs to room fourteen on the upper floor. We did not expect our accommodations to be plush. We did expect something comparable to an American economy motel. Instead, we found the beds covered in cheap, beige chenille spreads. At least, the bed clothing looked clean beneath them. The room had an unpainted wardrobe and nightstand, two brown-painted stool chairs and a red and white oilcloth-covered table. Brown-flowered curtains hung against green wallpaper with large pink flowers.

In another room, off the first, we found a bathtub and a lavatory, with "one of those things," a *bidet*, under the lavatory. I suspect one would scar their spine attempting to use it. The room did not contain a commode. We found the commode, which served the whole floor, out our door and down the hall on the left. Ruby declared she would not think of using it. The room containing the commode was very small, the width of the door.

Cliff had given me the name of friends in Paris if we really could not handle a situation. After our initial reaction and talking to one another, we decided to make the best of it. We would eat the fruit we bought in Zurich and go out for the afternoon. Then, certain to return before dark, we would lock ourselves in with the deadbolt and sleep the night.

When we went downstairs to go sightseeing, two young German girls were sitting in chairs in the lobby area. We exchanged greetings and learned that they were traveling like the Dunnam girls. After seeing them, I felt braver and safer. If they could do it, so could we! So, we went out into the rain-soaked street to find the Cityrama Tour office. We paid one hundred and fifty francs for our fares and went to await the bus on *Rue de Rivolia*. We were standing there in the rain until a tour guide saw us and came across the street to lead us to a shelter situated nearby to wait.

The three-hour tour took us all over Paris, while the rain continued without a break. We were glad to see it all from comfortable, dry seats on the upper deck of the bus. We had a choice of English for the earphones and were able to understand what we saw on the tour. We did fine except for French names.

As we rode along, Ruby asked, "Sybil, would you have done this trip alone?"

"No, Ruby, but with another fool to go along with you, you can do anything!"

We enjoyed the bright umbrellas of the pedestrians walking below us along the Seine. We were two middle-aged widows in Paris, who were not even sure we would ever get back to the "farm." How had we dared to do this? Embarked, there was nothing to do but to keep going. Truthfully, it never occurred to me that we might alter our plans and fly home. Already, I had wished for Don, or brother Shank, to be there to take care of things and us. Neither of us was a feminist. I thought gratefully of times Don or Shank ran interference for me. The tour days with Maxie Dunnam contrasted sharply to days on our own, when I had to do the legwork, figure out our course of action, keep tract of the money exchange, and make decisions. Maxie took care of the whole tour group for all the days of the tour.

When our city tour ended at 5 o'clock, we were pleased with our choice of activity for the afternoon and were very hungry. We found a cafeteria near our hotel and felt better after we had eaten the hearty food we found there. In a shop near where we had eaten, I found *eau de toilette* I liked. The clerk who sold me the fragrance asked for my silver TRY GOD Tiffany pin, given to me by a cousin. I refused to part with the pin. That may have been a *faux pas.* So be it.

Ruby went to bed as soon as we got back to the Golden Lion. I wrote a long letter to Ed and Kathey.

When we awoke on June 25, the rain had stopped and sun bathed our room in light. We had rested well and slept peacefully. The room looked much better to us than it had the day before. As we started to find breakfast, we met the little house cleaner bringing a tray with bread, jelly and coffee to us. We were happily surprised that our economy hotel provided a Continental breakfast. We followed her back to our oddly decorated room enjoy the hotel's hospitality.

Since our bus tour had followed the Seine the day before, we decided that we would forego the Seine River trip. Instead, we walked to the nearby *L'Ouvre* and found a long waiting line. Ruby commented on the nude statuary, which disturbed her moral sensibilities, on the lawn in front of the *L'Ouvre*. We had purchased our train tickets earlier and had planned to use that day for sightseeing. However, neither of us was keen on waiting, maybe in vain, to get into *L'Ouvre* and Ruby said, "I saw enough art in Rome to last the rest of my life."

So, that being settled, we went back to the hotel, where we had left our bags in the reception area, and asked the wife of the Spanish manager to call a taxi for us. Traffic was heavy, but we had lots of time. We decided to have a nice dinner at the train station, *Gare de Nord*, while we waited for our train to Amsterdam.

Trying to avoid having French francs left, we were not sure we had enough cash to cover our dinner. We gave the waiter an additional American dollar. He signaled it was all right. I also gave him an orange ballpoint pen from Orange Savings Bank of Chapel Hill, North Carolina. An experience years later in Europe makes me suspect the gratuity was included in the bill and that we over-tipped him.

By the time we finished dinner, we had only a short while to wait for the train. We shared our compartment in the train with a young student who spoke some English. He had visited in Connecticut and hoped to visit an uncle, who was the French general consul in Houston, Texas. After he left us, we had the compartment to ourselves until a little Belgian woman joined us. She was on her way to Antwerp and told us that she had been a widow for two years. We had widowhood in common. We became friends in that short while and she promised to pray for us. We needed her prayers.

CHAPTER XI

Amsterdam Rescue

We arrived in Amsterdam at 9:30PM. By the time, I was able to exchange money it had grown late. The line had been long. On our way to pick up our luggage, we passed a sad-looking inebriated fellow, who tried to attract our attention, to ask for money, I suppose. He had urinated where he sat.

My next concern was to reach Cliff, who was staying with a family in Tilburg. I needed to call him for instructions as to our next move. I found a phone near the railroad track, under the shelter. However, I could not get the number I was trying to call. I asked a conductor standing nearby by his train to help me. My coin caught in the telephone. The train would be leaving any minute. He banged the phone, the coin fell, and I caught my breath. His train was ready to go. I rang the number, and the person who answered called Cliff. I waved goodbye to my angel and sighed so deeply that I felt it echoed.

Cliff's hosts suggested we try the Hilton for our accommodation, and mentioned the Apollo. We had to sleep somewhere. By now it was nearly too late to get our bags out of the baggage room. Anxiety made me feel that my blood pressure was rising. Thankfully, the man behind the counter took mercy on me and gave me our bags.

After I explained our predicament, he even phoned the Hilton, which had no vacancies. Then he called the Apollo for us.

We felt blessed when the taxi driver we found could speak English. The hotel proved to be elegant and expensive. We must have looked shocked when the desk clerk e told us what it would cost to spend the night. He looked at the two of us, travel-worn as we were, and volunteered, "Perhaps you would like to find a less expensive hotel?"

We were exhausted! It seemed an eternity since seven o'clock in Paris that morning. We needed sleep and to wash our hair. No, we did not want to waste another minute. We were ready to pay whatever he might ask. We gratefully paid our nice taxi driver fifteen Dutch guilders and told him goodnight. Ruby and I had been traveling for twenty days.

People in Amsterdam were far more courteous and helpful than in Paris, except the man who had exchanged my money. He had a moneychanger attitude, no doubt! I excused him. The flesh gets weary after meeting the public all day long. Pressed all day by endless lines of people buying tickets, making reservations, asking information and struggling to understand the language difference must be wearing. Other than the money- man, Amsterdam received a high first impression rating from me.

It was not yet six when I awoke the morning of June 26, in spite of my not having gone to bed until 1:30 AM. Cliff expected me to call him from the hotel. I got him out of bed, so obviously he did not expect me to call at 7:20 AM. He said that he would come for us until after lunch. Since we had the morning to ourselves, we decided to go into the town again. After breakfast at the hotel, we checked out and asked permission to leave our bags in the hotel lobby until the afternoon. We went by the tram to Central Station in Amsterdam to purchase our tickets for the Boattrain to London the next day. There would be time enough for us to take the canal boat tour before going back to the hotel to meet Cliff and Mary.

Amsterdam is a very important seaport. To me the big city seemed dirty, bustling and without orderliness as we approached the boat on the canal. Our excursion by water gave us some flavor of the place and people. As we motored through the canals, we noticed cats on many of the boats and pigeons in crevices under the bridges. The houses along the canal reminded me of the row houses in Baltimore. They shared walls and had no lawns or flowers.

As we went back to the hotel by train, we were able to see the parts of the city through which we had passed the night before. We were walking back to our hotel from the train when we saw another hotel called Apollofirst. It was near the Hilton. Perhaps the baggage-man had called this hotel the night before. It was very near, only two stoplights from the Apollo, where Mary and Cliff were waiting for us.

Cliff took us to an Indonesian restaurant for delicious food, lots of food! By the time we had eaten most of it, it was 6 PM. Cliff drove us back to the train station to check our excess luggage. We only needed enough for the one night in Tilburg.

Cliff and I went in to check the bags, while Mary and Ruby stayed with the car. It felt wonderful to have Cliff take over and make the decisions. He knew his way around this strange place. I could rely on him. We stopped by the baggage room, on our way to make reservations, checked the bags and paid the fee.

We waited nearly two hours in line for reservations, only to learn that we could not make reservations. Workers were on strike. The English Boattrain would not run; the Dutch boat had no more room. Cliff went to retrieve the bags, while I waited in another line to obtain a refund for our tickets. Strangely, when Cliff went for our luggage the baggage room attendant did not know about the strike, which explained why he had accepted our bags earlier. Stranger still, when I asked for a refund, the ticket agent did not know about the strike either. She had been selling tickets for passages for a trip that would not be made. The one making reservations did know, and the ticket agent, who did not know, were in the same room, not more than fifteen feet apart. This seemed nightmarish, like one of my anxiety dreams.

Finally, we were free to drive to Tilburg. It was 10:30 PM. Cliff checked us into the Ibis Motel. I felt disappointed that we still had not heard from Andy. We all should have been together on this day that would have been Don's fifty-seventh birthday. I was afraid to ask Cliff why Andy had not come. Cliff was taking responsibility for all of us: Mary, Andy, Ruby and me. Could he handle it with humor?

The long day over, I wrote in my journal with nostalgia:

Dear Lord, what do you have in heaven in place of hugs and kisses? I am sure Don does not need them there with you. It probably does not matter at all, as it would if he were here, how much I love him. Are old birthdays forgotten in the greater remembrances of heaven? Fifty-seven years in the light of eternity must seem insignificance.

How do I assess thirty-three years, two months, eleven days that Don and I were man and wife? I am thankful for his love and that his love taught me something about the quality of your love. Dear Father, there are so many times his love was tested by my imperfections and outright insensitivity. Yet he continued to love me. Unlike you, Lord, he could be hurt or angered by what I did or said. He did not understanding any more perfectly than I do. I loved him as he loved me, imperfectly!

Lord, I do not mean to ask of you something I should not ask. I know you are God and are perfect everything. However, there is so much I do not know and understand. I need to learn acceptance and simply trust you. I am trying, because I want to trust you.

I know you understand because you are God. It should be enough to know that you are. Nevertheless, God, what am I to do with all this old leftover love hanging around my heart? What am I to do with the precious memories that only I can cherish? I shared them with Don and he no longer lives?

The first, difficult anniversary had arrived and passed. When I reread what I had written, it seemed that I had reached a point of acceptance. However, in the following months my feelings became more and more bizarre. On June 27, my journal entry indicates my confusion. I had a hard time sorting out my thoughts and feelings.

Journal entry: *Should I talk about Don or refrain from talking of him? Should I talk to Don in my mind as I did when he lived, trying to sort out differences and improve our understanding? Certainly, things I would have said to him about common concerns and temporal interests are futile now. He has no voice to answer me, nor hands to help me, even if he hears*

Jesus, are you, as you always have been, my Liaison? Not only between God and me, but between Don and me? Does death separate us, because he has ceased to be mortal, while my mortality remains? Alternatively, are we one in you, and therefore not separated, with no need of putting thoughts into words?

Andy arrived at the motel first thing next morning. Cliff had been called to play tennis and had gone back to get his clothes. Ruby decided not to go watch the tennis match, so Andy and I went downstairs. Andy knew the way. He and I began to walk, but Mary came in the car to take us to the indoor court. I did not understand my uneasiness as I sat watching Cliff play. I wanted to give Cliff my support by being there, but I did enjoy watching the match being played inside a building. After the match, we went back to join Ruby at the motel for lunch.

Tilburg, much smaller and cleaner than Amsterdam, is a nice town. Ruby, Andy and I walked on the streets while Mary ran, for running was her sport. Cliff went for a haircut. By the time we got to the middle of town where there would be something to see, we decided we had rather be warm. Besides, it began to rain. We were glad when Mary and Cliff came in the car to pick us up and take us to the dry motel.

That evening, we gathered at the motel for dessert and coffee and visited awhile, but said goodnight early. Cliff was to take Ruby and me to the airport for an early flight to London, and we would have the motel call us early.

Next morning, Ruby and I went down at 7 AM for breakfast and had just finished when Andy, Cliff and Mary arrived. We were quickly on our way. After stopping for gas, Cliff drove very fast and we pulled into *Skipol* at 9 AM to pick up our reservations, which Cliff called and made for us. We went immediately to the boarding area for a security check. That required a bit of time. It was hard to say goodbye. My emotions were rocky as we left the airport on our 10 AM flight. We arrived in London at 10 AM, getting back an hour, because we were in a different time zone.

The enormous London airport teemed with people. A woman, in the bright colors and dress of India, who sat near us, overheard me remark to Ruby about the crowd. "You should see Calcutta," she said.

We went the breadth and length of all three terminals at least three times before we found where we needed to be. The underground tunnels reminded me of the catacombs in Rome. After several futile attempts at other hotels, I obtained a reservation at the Sheraton Heathrow. We were happy for the courtesy bus and the closeness of the motel. By the time we could check in, at 2:30 PM, both Ruby and I were exhausted. She took a nap while I wrote Mary, Cliff and Andy.

When Ruby awakened, we took the bus back to the airport and took the underground to central London. Most shops were closing by then. We walked on Haymarket, Piccadilly Circus, and Regent Street, had dinner at a Chinese restaurant, bought some fruit and took the underground back to our motel. Ruby called Hatteras--a world away. Her son gave her news of her aged mother and told her that he and his family were getting ready to go the Austin Reunion. Ruby and I were going to bed in London, tired and homesick, looking forward to June 30 and going home. I wanted to be at my family's reunion. However, I did not want to be there without Don, Andy, and Cliff. Would Ed and Kathey be at the reunion, which is held every two years. Except for my brother Shank, my siblings and their families and mine had attended the first Austin Reunion in 1978. I went to bed to sleep and forget.

CHAPTER XII

London, England

We began our London day with worship at St. George's Interdenominational Chapel at Heathrow Airport, where we received communion from the Church of England chaplain. I felt privileged to be there. I moved toward a small, weeping, dark-skinned girl. My own wounded heart made me sensitive to her tears. I took her, my sister in Christ, into my arms. When she smiled, I knew my action had been right. She accepted my expression of love. God knew our hearts—hers and mine.

Ruby and I left the chapel to browse around the airport shops before returning to the hotel. There, we decided to eat breakfast, since they were still serving at 11:30 AM. Our two-hour bus tour of downtown London would not begin until 2:30 PM.

The London sightseeing tour did not measure up to our Paris experience. It is not that London is less charming. With its bobbies and uniformed, red-coated guards of Buckingham Palace, it has as much to offer as Paris. There are many famous landmarks to appreciate along the Thames River. Language did not separate us from our travel guide. But I felt frustrated and angry when we reached points of interest before the guide alerted us to what we should see. Was it the fault of the bus driver or our inattentiveness? Did he take us beyond the viewpoint too quickly?

The Wimbledon sign along our route caused me nostalgic regret. We were tired and ready to go home. Perhaps our mood influenced the last day of our European excursion.

The only time we actually stopped and got out of the bus was at what had been a tobacco shop, which now stood empty. The driver told us that The Old Curiosity Shop was thought to be the oldest shop in that part of London. Built in 1567, it was one of the few buildings to survive the Great Fire of London in 1666, even though constructed of wood from ships. Victorian-era writer Charles Dickens (1812-1870) immortalized the shop in a novel by the same name. The tour director shared that there was hope of preserving the "shop of trinkets and curious things" that intrigued Dickens, for historical reasons. On the Internet (about. com: London Travel), I learned that in September of 2008 The Old Curiosity Shop became home to the Blaak Boutique.

After our tour, we walked around to the other side of Russell Square. We went into The British Museum and looked at some exhibits, i.e., statues of Buddha, woodcarvings from different Eastern cultures and artifacts from Egypt. The handwriting of the two authors named Browning, Shelley, and other writers interested me. However, we were half-hearted in our interest. Everything seemed anticlimactic. We were just keeping ourselves busy to pass the time until we could board our plane for home.

When we came out of the museum, we were in unfamiliar territory and felt very lost. Two Swiss women had a map and one tried to direct us, but we felt her directions were faulty. We thought her map might be upside-down. Unsure, we were making another inquiry of an elderly man, who began to direct us, when a matronly woman arrived and assumed responsibility.

"I've helped three other people, I might as well help you," she declared matter-of-factly and with authority. She claimed us for her own, took my arm, and began to propel me along the sidewalk. Her brown eyes danced. She began to sing a little song about helping others.

"My name is Phyllis," she said "Do you know anything about reincarnation?"

"Not much," I answered, as we hurried along.

"I've been a man six times, a woman six times, and three other times I don't know which sex I was," she said.

Ruby's facial expression showed her disdain for both the subject and the speaker. Ruby walked ahead, signaling me to leave Phyllis.

Even though I was looking for a chance in the conversation to break away from the woman, I did not want to reject her. Phyllis' story and point of view interested me, and there was a possibility that I might have an opportunity to share my faith in Christ with her.

Ruby, who stood unhappily farther up the block, did not look at all supportive. I knew she doubted my ability to influence Phyllis. Finally, I did attempt to speak of my faith to her, and I managed to interrupt her stories of her former lives to join Ruby.

As we walked along the sidewalk on our way to the underground transportation system to go back to the hotel, Ruby said, "I wish you had a boyfriend to go with you to see the plays." I had expressed a desire to see one of the plays, "Oliver" or "My Fair Lady," which were playing in London that week, but Ruby was not interested.

"That would be nice!" I chuckled falsely. In my innermost heart, I whispered, *Wish you were here, Honey!*

It was time to eat, so in spite of Cliff's advice to try the foods of the countries we visited and not rely on fast-food fare, we found a McDonald's to enjoy London's version of hamburger, chips and Coca Cola. The combinations did not taste the same as American French fries and coke.

On our last day in London, we read that Texas was having a heat wave—113 degrees—and some people had died. And, oh yes, there had been an earthquake in California. In spite of the bad news, we were counting the hours until our flight home.

I will never again be as ignorant as I was in 1980. Foreign travel is a huge undertaking, and I admire those who take it in stride. I pride myself on having done what Ruby and I did, but I will be even happier to rely on tour directors and guides hereafter. Still, I loved the adventure and risks we took.

I did not know if I would ever want to return to Europe. Grief and pain prejudiced each day and every happening during the weeks we traveled. Would it be easier, or not as easy, at home with friends?

Memories of our trip, and of Ruby's lifelong nap habit being pitted against the European places and events, make me smile. We missed much that we might have seen or done in order to accommodate her naps. We acquired a few special things when we shopped. Traveling took us to new places and experiences. Different cultures, languages, and people challenged us. Being abroad had broadened us.

Before we checked out of the hotel that last morning, Ruby and I had our devotions; then, breakfast at the Sheraton-Heathrow coffee shop before going over to the airport. We obtained our boarding passes right away. Then, we went to the duty-free shops to spend what we had left of our pounds sterling. The cost of a lovely white wool cardigan with dainty embroidered roses took the last of mine. Our pocketbooks were empty of foreign currency. We were ready to return home (where spending money was much easier) for what might await us there.

CHAPTER XIII

Coming Home to Chapel Hill

As we flew toward Boston, we had snacks and watched a movie, without sound. Without earphones, it was a challenge to understand what was happening in the drama of a Marine officer and his family. I identified with each in turn—a young boy and his love of basketball, the sister reveling in her first poem, the mother as she tried to keep all the relationships on an even keel.

Our plane did not land immediately after we reached our Boston destination. We thought the late landing was due to delayed boarding in London. That was a false assumption. We learned the reason as events unfolded after we landed in Boston. There was a reason the plane did not land when we arrived at our destination. When our plane landed, we were instructed to remain seated and to wait for the signal light before attempting to retrieve our overhead luggage. Before the light came on, three police officers came aboard and led a dark-eyed man with brown hair, mustache and glasses from the plane. Was he a terrorist, a stowaway, a fugitive from justice? We never learned.

We were home again. Now Ruby and I had to part. An American man we met at Heathrow Airport promised to help Ruby find the Allegheny Terminal for her flight to Norfolk. We boarded a shuttle bus amid thunder and lightening, and Ruby and the man disembarked first. I proceeded to the Piedmont terminal, where only a few people were waiting. I called the MacMillans in Hudson and Beth Skakle at Wareham. The terminal was so cold that I put on everything I could find in my hand luggage. I felt the health of babies and older adults waiting in the frigid terminal were in jeopardy. I read to pass the time but soon grew tired of reading. It was a long wait. Due to the storm, my flight left an hour later than scheduled.

When I arrived at Raleigh-Durham airport, I felt a terrible dread knowing there would be no one at my home to greet me. My heart was colder than the Piedmont Airlines waiting area had been. Merle Sykes and June Spruyt, neighbor-friends I expected to meet me, were not at the airport. Not sure if they had been there earlier and already left, not wanting to be stranded, I left for Chapel Hill in the airport limousine. They arrived at the airport 10 minutes after my limousine had left.

Feeling vulnerable and lonely, I asked the driver to take me home instead of leaving me at The Carolina Inn, which was the normal drop-off point. He kindly agreed to do that. Allen Spruyt, a young friend who fed the dogs for me while I was away, and his friend Gary Johnson were standing outside when we drove up to my house. They came to help with my bags. When I stepped onto the porch, I saw a sign by the light of the streetlight--a big yellow sign: WELCOME HOME, Sybil

When I read the signatures of some of my closest friend from my church, I burst into tears. Emotion engulfed me like a sudden, drenching rain. I said goodnight to the boys and greeted the two dogs around my feet, but the dogs would not enter the house, then or later -- not even for petting or food. Nikki, a white Spitz, liked the cold, even the snow. She would find a place in the snow near an oak tree in the back yard and would curl up and sleep there. Our Suki, with a black face like a Pekingese and long tan and white fur, had sat by Don's chair for his hand to find her ears. After his death, she stayed outside too. Perhaps she waited for him or disliked the grief she sensed in the house. Had the dogs been in the house, my aloneness would have been less acute.

I went inside and closed the door, and the silence and emptiness affronted me like a presence. It had been 24 hours since I had slept. I started not to make up the bed--our bed--but decided I had better do it right. I turned on the radio to listen to a local minister give a devotion, then crawled into bed. Tears, regrets, anguished questions that had no answers came uninvited into my mind; questions I did not want to ask lurked in the darkness, and I cried aloud, *Oh, Don, I need you so desperately!*

I had been away from home for 24 days. For that time, I half expected life would be good again. With activities planned for every day with loving people, it had not been too difficult. The house was very quiet except for the sounds of the air conditioner and refrigerator. I lay quietly in bed anticipating sleep. A sudden house sound, all houses have them, startled me. Physically and emotionally spent, I finally slept, hoping that I would feel braver and stronger after a good night's sleep.

Eddie called me first thing the next morning to welcome me home and to tell me he had a badly sprained ankle. Then he told me the real reason he called: that his marriage -- his relationship with Kathy --was troubled. His message jarred me back to the reality that life is. No longer a tourist in a foreign land, I had returned to a world of conflict and pain--others' and mine.

CHAPTER XIV

Probate and Taxes

The first night after Don's funeral, I was sitting in the living room when I heard a crash in the bedroom. I went to investigate and saw the contents of Don's top dresser drawer scattered on the floor. Eddie was trying to retrieve the contents of the drawer and Cliff was trying to put the drawer back in place. Kathey was crouched on the floor, sopping up shaving lotion that had fallen off the top of the dresser and was eating at the finish on the floor, with a handful of Don's clean white handkerchiefs, which Don always seemed to have available when my emotions caused tears. I made sure he had plenty available.

"What in the world are you doing? What are you looking for?" I asked. Why were my children bothering Don's things without even asking me?

"Mom, we're looking for a will," Cliff said. "Daddy said he always wrote, before he left on a trip, to say what he wanted to be done if something should happen to him. Have you seen one?"

Wills? Don and I had not made wills. Like Scarlett in *Gone with the Wind*, we kept planning to "think about it tomorrow." We had no sense of urgency. We had not written wills. Our tomorrow, that Scarlett talked of, came too soon.

"Would it be in his office at Woollen Gym, maybe?" Cliff asked.

Something was jamming the drawer. Cliff pulled it back out and reached far back into the opening to find out why it would not slide in easily. He found a couple of folded sheets of paper. He unfolded them. One was a poem Don's father had mailed to him, something he thought Don might use for a tennis team pep talk. The other was Don's hand-written will. He had written it before we left Chapel Hill to drive to Maine five years earlier, to celebrate Poppa Skakle's eightieth birthday. Don's brother and family lived in Stockton Springs, Maine, and Poppa Skakle and Beth were visiting them.

The holographic will covered the eventuality of our dying together in an automobile accident. If so, everything was to be divided equally among our three sons. Thankfully, Don had added that if he died first, I was to be his sole beneficiary.

Kathey, an only child whose father had died years earlier, acted as administrator for her mother's estate in 1979 and knew what we needed to do first. The next day we took the will to the Orange County clerk of court. Andy was not available, but Eddie, Kathey and Cliff went with me to attest to the will and the validity of the signature. The clerk appointed me legal administrator of the estate, and probate began.

I obtained letters of testament, which allowed me access to our savings and checking accounts. Even though we had them in joint tenancy, at death half became frozen until legal restraints were satisfied.

When I applied for North Carolina Teacher's Retirement Plan benefits from Don's account, I learned that Don had not changed the beneficiary status of his account since the first year he began teaching in 1950, when we had only one son. In order for me to receive the benefits under a pension arrangement, with a monthly check, our oldest son, Donald Edmund Skakle, Jr., had to sign over his claim to half of the benefits. Otherwise, the benefit would have been a lump sum, divided between Eddie and me, with no regard for Andy and Cliff.

I believe that Don trusted me and knew that I would always be concerned for the welfare of our sons and that I would treat them fairly and equitably. I do not doubt that Don meant to do that too. Recalling my own father's final letter to his children, I regretted that my sons did not have the satisfaction of knowing by his written word and a will how Don, their father, thought of them. The suddenness of his death had left all of us wanting for assurance. For weeks, for months, I searched in unlikely places for a goodbye message from him to me.

Having started probate before leaving for Europe, I withdrew funds and repaid Mona the money she loaned me for the trip reservations. Now, back from my trip, the probate and related legalities needed my attention. I had a good friend, Olga Morrison, who knew about taxes. Don and I had employed her to do our taxes for the past few years. Olga took responsibility for filing the first tax forms and coached me through the rest.

It took several months to file all the claims for insurance monies. Neither Don nor I owned large insurance premiums. In fact, I had none at all. Don's from the university was the largest, and the young woman who worked in the university benefits department called to tell me that my benefits were less than she first quoted to me. I did not question that until later, when I learned from a friend who worked in the University of North Carolina accounting office that insurance did not cover Don's complete salary. Don worked under two administrators, physical education and athletics, receiving a salary from each department. However, a university rule required that the two salaries combined should not exceed the salary amount of other faculty members of his same rank. Don's rank was that of associate professor, and most of his income came from the physical education department. His athletic salary was considerably lower than the one from the physical education department.

When I began to question why his total salary was not covered, I became angry. A determination fortified by anger and grief made me feel that I must defend his rights. Therefore, I wrote Trisha Hunt, North Carolina government representative, and made an appointment with John Temple, vice chancellor of the University of North Carolina, to discuss the matter.

Another burning concern that had been Don's now became mine—an indoor tennis facility. Don promoted this cause widely and sought financial backing among the tennis crowd for years prior to his death. He fought for it within the administration and suffered disappointment, year after year.

I made an appointment to see Athletic Director John Swofford. He had a model in his office of what was to become Dean Smith Basketball Center. Since the on-campus tennis courts had been taken for the building of The Paul Green Theater, tennis playing had been relegated to courts distant from the center of campus, and tennis had lost most of its following. Interest had waned. Don had agonized over this. The courts, which were constructed on property acquired from the Old Chapel Hill Country Club, were hard to find and off the beaten path. Prior to the building of the courts at that site, the team had sometimes played on tennis courts behind Hinton James dormitory. It was supposed that those courts were to be destroyed in preparation for the construction of Dean Dome. I proposed the Hinton James Courts be preserved and that, for the convenience of fans of both sports, Carolina's indoor tennis facility be planned and built near Dean Dome. The better location would help promote tennis, and one parking area would serve both basketball and tennis. Mr. Swofford called me the next week to say the request for the tennis complex was submitted. (However, it did not receive funding at that time.)

The site of the tennis complex built later and dedicated in 1992 is even less accessible than the old location. Cone-Kenfield Tennis Center, hidden in the woods behind the Friday Convention Center off Route 54, is accessible by a long, narrow, winding road, far from the center of the UNC campus, and requires a vehicle of some sort to get there.

A former team member gave money for a court in the new

complex to be named for Don. A road leading to the complex is named Skakle Drive. These do not compensate for the devotion he gave to Carolina and the honor his service brought to Carolina tennis. What does balance Don Skakle's ledger is the love and respect of former UNC tennis team members he coached, of students he taught, and of friends who remember him I am grateful for these.

My efforts with Vice Chancellor Temple were more positive than with Swofford. He investigated and found that, while the insurance award was not based on Don's total salary, his pension benefits were correct. My belief is that an additional amount of money I received represented the full amount of the insurance award. I felt I had done *something* to right wrongs.

Money, money, money! How our lives depend on it and revolve around it. In spite of our wanting it not to be an idol, its necessity requires we spend much time to acquire it and more to take care of what we have.

Probate went smoothly and taxes were paid. I found the estate taxes very offensive. Taxes take a large part, more and more, of our earnings while we live. It seems immoral, even obscene, that when someone dies, the "wolves" scratch at the door for more. My vote is to eliminate the death tax forever. Would a constitutional amendment help?

I had more financial capital after Don's death than we ever had when he lived. I followed a friend's advice and invested the remainder of the insurance award in the stock market. Financial security is a blessing, and I felt fortunate for my employment and for my inheritance. I thanked God for the financial, professional, physical and spiritual resources that were available to me. I was blessed and am. Yet, in spite of my security, I felt poor and afraid.

CHAPTER XV

Professional Help

"In America the first significant studies concerning human psychology as it pertains to grief appeared in the early 1940's. Only in the last two generations have scientists gathered systematic information about the processes of human adjustment pertaining to bereavement." (*Living through Personal Crisis* by Ann Kaiser Sterns, 1984, The Thomas More Press, Chicago)

Even though such studies exist, industry and organizations, as well as individuals, have been slow in learning about them. Perhaps it is not surprising that Durham County General Hospital considered three days sufficient time for bereavement in 1980.

Kaiser Sterns wrote, "Great tragedies are more likely to require professional help because the wake is high after an enormous ship passes."

Andy expressed concern for me and I allowed him to call Dr. Earl Somers, a psychiatrist, and make an appointment for the evening before I left for Europe. I do not know what Andy observed in my behavior that prompted him to suggest it.

I knew Dr. Somers as a writer. He had been one of my classmates when I attended a short-story writing course in night classes at UNC in 1964. Dr. Somers had an excellent reputation as a psychiatrist in Chapel Hill and at the UNC Medical School.

He agreed to meet Andy and me that evening. While I felt grateful that he would, I felt uncomfortable for asking him to see me after hours. However, I was due to fly to Boston, on my way to Rome and other points, the next morning. It had to be then.

Immediately after Don's death, I had attended a seminar on grief, conducted by a pastor of the United Methodist Church. He had defined the stages of grief. I probably thought that knowing the stages by name would help me handle them and told myself that I was going to see Dr. Somers for Andy's sake

Andy went with me and waited for me. I felt unsure and anxious as Dr. Somers ushered me into his office. I sat near the door with a box of tissues close by. A tall, slender, well-dressed man, Dr. Somers loosened his tie and sat down near his desk in the armed desk chair to my right. He crossed right leg over left knee and relaxed to listen, putting me at ease by his actions of relaxation. Our first session began.

Andy had moved back home to live with Don and me in December before Don's death. I feared that I could not handle, or was badly coping with Andy's failed marriage, his loss of job, and his prospects of finding one. Committed to leaving for Europe the next morning, I felt reluctant to leave Andy and wanted to ask Dr. Somers about my dread. At times, he creased his brow as he listened and volunteered little in the way of advice.

Over the years, I have heard people poke fun at psychiatrists. I knew that many still considered those who go to psychiatrists suspect. I considered myself enlightened by books I had read and personal knowledge of the good that psychiatrists accomplish. I had heard some Christian friends express the opinion that only a Christian psychiatrist can help a Christian. Therefore, I asked, "Are you a Christian?"

He countered by inquiring about the depth of my faith and asked how I expressed my devotion to God. On the defensive, I tried to explain my beliefs to him. I told him that I sought to follow Christ's teachings and his commandments to love God and neighbor, that being Christian was more about belief in Christ as

Savior than it was about behavior. I affirmed that with all others who claim Christ, I journey toward becoming like Christ and recognized God's love and the truth inherent in evangelist Tommy Lewis' statement: "God hates sin because it hurts the sinner, whom God loves."

Therefore, I thought it wise to follow God's instructions for behavior set forth in the Ten Commandments. To be obedient to them protected me from being hurt or from hurting others. To love God with all my heart, mind, and strength and treat all I met as worthy of my love and respect took care of the "dos and don'ts" of the religions of all the cultures of the world. I hoped to not be the victim of lies, theft, envy, adultery, and disrespect, or to inflict others by breaking God's laws.

Loving God and others, as God loves me, is not easy. My ego is so much a part of who I am. To surrender to love when I had rather defend myself goes against my selfish human nature. Yet, I desire to please God by my surrender and dependence on him.

As Andy and I started to leave, Dr. Somers said, "Sybil, if you had a good friend to listen, you would probably be fine. However, I think it would be worth investment of your time and money to let me help you work through your grief. When you come back from Europe, we can plan a series of appointments, if you decide it is what you want to do."

I had no plan to set up appointments with Dr. Somers when I left his office in June. I finally called him in November, and on November 7 we set up a series of appointments in which he listened attentively while I sorted out my feelings, dealt with my terrible anger, and came to accept Don's death and my singleness.

Part of grief is "if only" moments. I had several of those: If only I had been available to Don, to listen and to help relieve his stress; if only we had been less busy.

Dr. Somers reminded me that I could not have listened unless Don had been there to talk, and that he might not have talked even if I had been there to listen. I knew that was true. That truth shot down that "if only" as if it were one of those creatures in a video game.

When Don and I had shopped at Sears the Saturday before Christmas, it was satisfying and appreciated because we were together and making decisions about the gifts for our sons. A weekend visit to a cousin in Norfolk in February had been our first weekend together, without job responsibilities, in months. I could claim only half the blame for any separation of ours. I was never responsible for more than half of the relationship!

As we progressed in my sessions with Dr. Somers, I began to air complaints against Don. I discounted his thoughtful, unselfish, loving acts toward our sons and me, while I charged him for all the times he failed me. After one bitter outpouring of anger, I asked Dr. Somers, "What's wrong with me?"

"You're grieving," Dr. Somers said.

I did not believe he could be right. I seethed with spiteful venom. How could bitterness, devoid of affection, be grief?

Then, Dr. Somers asked, "Why do you feel guilty?"

I took that one home. Why did I feel guilty? Was my anger an indication that I felt guilty? I wondered if Dr. Somers thought I had been unfaithful or felt I had contributed to Don's death by being mean and spiteful. Neither was true!

I wrote a letter to Dr. Somers, trying to answer his question, after I questioned myself. Did I betray Christ's admonition to love others as he loves me by my unloving and vengeful thoughts? I could accept that reason for guilt. I was guilty.

Dr. Somers never discussed the letter with me; never told me if he agreed that my guilt was due to my failure to love.

I examined the positive aspects of my marriage and the character of the man I had called husband to write that letter. We were imperfect, he and I. In spite of our disagreements and different viewpoints, our marriage had endured losses, disappointments, and struggles. We both enjoyed hard work and worked together better than we played. He worked tirelessly at the tennis he played.

As I processed the information, I concluded I could forgive Don for his imperfections.

After I let Don off the hook, I put myself on the scaffold and tried to execute Sybil. Thinking I had succeeded in unsettling "if only," vain regret, its mirror image self-condemnation, consumed me.

At another session, Dr. Somers asked, "Why do you torment yourself?"

Again, I had to retreat and think about that. I did not recognize my self-judgment and condemnation as torture. Finally, I decided I did not deserve such treatment. Forgiving Don compelled me to forgive myself. It happened as I drove alone one day. When I realized I could chose to elect or reject self-disparaging thoughts toward myself, I laughed aloud and said to the empty interior of the car: "I don't deserve to be tortured." Thereby, I forgave myself and became a loving woman again.

These liberations convinced me that psychiatry is one of God's means to free me from the untruth of my own devising. My time in therapy with Dr. Somers gave me a greater appreciation for God's character. God listens to me as Dr. Somers did, without condemnation of even my most negative and most odious thoughts. Both God and Dr. Somers accepted me as friend, with all my ugliness. When I told Dr. Somers in anger, "You don't even listen to what I say," he did not defend himself. He left it up to me to decide whether he was enemy or friend. Nor did he weigh my decisions by looking hurt or angry.

Whether Dr. Somers heard all I said or not, he cared that I should make good choices. His steady good will helped me process and discard old attitudes that hampered my love of others and of self. Had he thought a reprimand would help me out of my shackles, I believe he would have given one. He rightly assessed that I most needed affirmation and reassurance, which he gave me without being untruthful or sentimental.

Friends could have listened, and some did. My pastor would have heard me, but because I was so angry at Don, I felt like a traitor when I talked to him once. Paying for a professional's time, knowing he would listen and not judge either Don or me, enabled me to be truthful and kept me from feeling disloyal to Don. We fear reproach from one another, but the emotions and behaviors we hide, fearing rejection, do not shock psychiatrists. A good psychiatrist is an instrument of healing—God's merciful provisions for man and his soul. A good psychiatrist is a gift from God.

During therapy, I considered some of my vivid dreams. After relating one, I asked Dr. Somers, "What does it mean?"

"You wrote the script. What do you think it means?" he asked.

I recorded some of my dreams and tried to untangle the strange strands. One of them, in which I saw a slender, young woman, struggling to unzip the back of her long, sleek, black evening gown, seemed easy to interpret.

"All right," she said irritably, "I'll wear this for six months. After that I mean to be done with mourning."

Swiss psychiatrist Carl Jung called the unrecognizable people in our dreams "shadows." Whether male or female, these strangers represent us and reveal aspects of our personalities. In the shrug of her shoulders, in her attitude of defiance, I recognized myself. She did not look like me. However, that dream was about me. I hated being a widow.

In many of my dreams, I was trying to find my car, lost keys, or a lost purse. Sometime I would be trying to get to work or to get back home without a car. I would run and run and run to get there. The theme seemed to be loss of security. Anxiety was the emotion. Systematically, I had to assume responsibility for myself.

I came to rely on my sessions with Dr. Somers each week. Interaction with friends at work, at church, and in the community helped, too. One time, when Dr. Somers called me at work to cancel our appointment, I was undone; I felt abandoned. Fortunately, I attended a healing seminar session at a downtown church that day. The speaker's subject was anger. Only two or three people in the congregation raised their hands when the speaker asked, "How many of you handle your anger without guilt?"

I was one who felt guilty when I experienced anger. I did not raise my hand. I gained greatly by understanding that anger is part of an array of human emotions that enrich our personalities. The speaker explained that we love more intensely when we have a nature that is subject to anger. Anger against injustice and unrighteousness are very positive emotions. "Jesus," she said, "told us to be angry."

I knew that Scripture. The speaker's discourse helped me understand that anger can be a positive part of who I am. To be angry is not sinful. It is not even shameful. It is part of the human personality, a reflection of God's own nature.

Jesus' complete directive was, "Be angry and sin not." The speaker helped me understand that I should acknowledge my anger, exert self-control, and practice wisdom in expressing the anger, always seeking to maintain personal integrity. I learned that I promote my own spiritual growth when I channel my anger to serve God, to defend others, to practice self-control, and to avoid turning my anger against another or myself.

Dr. Somers agreed that the seminar had been God's providence for me, taking the place of my appointment with him. It was a blessing indeed!

Medication Dr. Somers prescribed helped alleviate the anxiety and stress that were part of those first months. I think his reaction to my having taken an anti-depressant Don had left indicated that he feared I might overdose. "You are not to take anything unless I tell you, and no more than I say," he said sternly.

He prescribed the same medication I had taken, at one-half the dose. The anti-depressant helped eliminate unpleasant sensations in my arms, which I attempted to jest about, "According to the marriage ceremony, two become one. It feels to me like Don is oozing out the pores of my arms."

However, the sensations were disturbing and uncomfortable—not at all amusing. I did not take the medication regularly. When my supply got low, I held off taking one until I felt a great need to be calm and focused. Being a pharmacist, I knew the drug. I did not intend to become dependent on anything that would hamper my complete recovery.

Something I did, which Dr. Somers had not suggested, helped very much: I joined a health spa. Two or three times a week, I went to exercise and swim. Exertion helped my sense of well-being, helped release stress in my body and emotions and improved my self-image. I continued for a year.

I had acquitted Don and freed myself from blame, but then I turned my anger toward God. One late afternoon, leaving work to face another lonely, joyless, desolate evening at home, I reached a new depth of despair. The car seemed a haven where I could let go and cry. It may not have been the safest place. However, after the day's work ended, I found tears came unheeded. That afternoon I took God to task:

"You are impotent! Don would not have died if you were omnipotent. If you are not omnipotent, you are not God," I sobbed.

At that moment, I doubted the existence of God. However, I had only driven out of the parking lot and was waiting for the light to turn green at the corner of Roxboro Road and Stadium Drive—less than a block—when I realized my utter dependence on God. I remembered how he had provided for me by the care from my family and my friends. Although my pain remained, I had strength to live and to work in spite of it. My tears stopped. I remembered days when hope prevailed and I felt truly interested in something or someone else. As the light changed, I brushed away my tears and cried aloud, "Oh, God, I could not have lived these months had you not been with me. Forgive me for doubting you. Thank you, Lord."

By the end of the first year, I saw Dr. Somers less often. Part of my therapy had been having the opportunity to recognize and deal with childhood issues. That was an unexpected bonus.

Therapy convinced me of the wisdom of seeking help when

and if I should have trouble with relationships, personal conflicts, or my emotions in the future. Why should I not seek a psychiatrist's help? With persistent indigestion or a broken leg, I would seek an internist or an orthopedic doctor, the sooner the better. Each specialist is available to help me. Many suffer needlessly because they are reluctant to seek help. I have heard the retort, "I'm not crazy. Why should I see a psychiatrist?"

Those "not crazy" respond most readily to therapy. Likewise, a simple fracture will heal more quickly than a compound fracture. A truly deranged mind, except for a miracle, takes many, many months of treatment. A fracture involving damage of surrounding tissue and injury to blood vessels, when the bone breaks through the skin, will require more care to repair and take longer to heal. To disregard injuries, whether physical or emotional, invites complications and longer recovery time. An unset bone may result in a permanent limp or deformity. Injuries to the psyche cause neurosis or worse mental distortions.

I am grateful for the availability of physicians for physical and emotional care. I am grateful for friends, who provided more attention than I could afford from a professional. Spa, seminars, trips, interests, happenings kept me moving toward a future I felt obligated to challenge, whether I wanted to or not.

CHAPTER XVI

Physical Want-
Sexuality

Raising three sons with Don, I had practical experience in coping and managing in assorted circumstances and situations. However, having Don to back me up, to lend counsel, to help make decisions, and to provide physical assistance always made me braver and bolder. My emotional security depended on Don's physical availability, even though I was not dependent on him.

When Don's coaching responsibilities took him away from home, I kept very busy. Busyness made time pass faster. His evening phone calls bridged the miles between us and were the highlight of my day, enabling us to share the events and express our love for one another in words. I never slept soundly when I awaited his return. The sound of his key in the door was my cue. I leapt from bed, rushed to the door, eager to have his arms hold and reassure me that he was safe and home again. The sight of him, his scent, his voice, his arms around me and his lips on mine fed deep hungers and gave me affirmation. Without him, I felt like a puzzle with pieces missing. I did not take his love for granted. I prized our life together. I enjoyed his company, the stories he shared, and physical union with him.

Sexuality is a part of who I am. Trusting no one to give me answers except God, casual, secular, simplistic solutions did not satisfy me. God created us male and female. Only God has the true answer to the riddles and misunderstandings that are abroad about our mysterious sexuality.

Popular magazines are intent on selling magazines, not in giving a balanced view of human sexuality. The media's use of sex to sell everything from soap to mattresses is offensive. The absence of, or disregard of, moral guidelines for sexuality creates social problems, both physical and psychological. In this age of enlightenment, the cost of sexual misconduct and ignorance adds a great burden of debt to society.

Sexuality is a precious gift from God—underappreciated in an age we call enlightened. Sexuality figures into the society and culture of every country, city, household, and individual. Every organization and business must acknowledge and deal with the problems sexuality may cause. It is subject to abuse and excesses that change that which God intended to be the expression of love and affirmation between a man and a woman to something ugly, exploitive, and hurtful. The sexual equation is complicated, difficult, and troubling in good ways and in bad ways. Renown psychiatrist Sigmund Freud made sexuality the basis of his theory of psychoanalysis.

A statement I read as a member of Academy for Spiritual Formation (1994-95) startled me: "There is no spirituality aside from sexuality." Of course, every person is both spiritual and sexual. Individuals decide the limits and expression of their spirituality and their sexuality. As a Christian widow, I seek to live with my sexuality and my spirituality in balance. God's faithfulness to me and mine to him require that I value my integrity in all facets of my life. Therefore, I use the knowledge and means God provides for me to live a healthy, moral life.

While this is not an easy subject to write about, to disregard it would be a mistake. Sexuality is involved in grief. Adapting to the physical and emotional losses is punishing. Sexual appetite is as real and natural as other physical and emotional needs. It is part of our human physical and emotional need. Appetite and thirst for food and water continue even when water and food are not available.

Having enjoyed many good years of sexual intimacy and partnership with my husband, when I found myself alone at fifty-four, I struggled with my sexuality. Experience had helped me understand my needs. Left alone, I felt sexuality a burden. Babies have a need to be held and cuddled. Puppies and kittens like to loll against one another. My mind, spirit, and body hungered for Don.

July 12, 1980, journal entry:

I slept well, but awakened with a great physical hunger. I have compassion for singles, who have no one to share their lives and themselves.

This morning my body is a burden to my soul, as it has been so many times. There must be many thousands like I am, locked into situations for various reasons, who feel as I do and are unable to express their sexuality.

To have a body full of desire for someone loved without hope of fulfillment is like not having God to praise and adore. For the mortal that I am, it seems worse. How do those who vow to celibacy decide that God is enough?

Early in life, I discovered the mystery of orgasm but did not know its name or its connection to my sexuality. By the time I started dating, I better understood my sexual urges. Masturbation provided a release from the sexual tension of hormonal changes, menstrual cycle, and outside stimuli, and helped me keep my vow to remain a virgin until married.

Some of my generation regard masturbation as wrong and may be as ignorant as I was and not even know its name. Sex was a taboo subject. But as I came to the age of awareness, I concluded that masturbation, even if questionable, was safer than sexual activity with another. I hurt no one else by my action. It kept me from becoming victim to another's sexual appetite and them from becoming victim of mine. I was a freshman in college when I accidentally discovered the definition of masturbation in the dictionary.

A mother wrote Ann Landers to express her horror upon finding her teenage son engaged in masturbation. Landers reassured her that it is normal and advised her to get help to explore her own misconceptions about the act.

I do not know about today's youth, but my friends and I did not talk about our sexual feelings. Our conversations centered on verbal intercourse: "He said. and I said to him." We had rules we followed in dating. Kissing was permitted, but within limits. Keeping the rules helped keep passion under control. Fair or not, we girls accepted the greater responsibility for keeping the rules. Girls should act as referees, for they risk the most. Due to their vulnerability, they should avoid alcohol and other substances that dull reactions and cloud their reason.

When former U.S. Surgeon General Joycelyn Elders talked about masturbation, President Clinton asked her to resign. She did. However, during an interview on a local talk show (WUNC-FM), Dr. Elders stood her ground. She did not alter her opinions supporting masturbation: "Ninety percent of all American males masturbate, and about seventy percent of all females, so pretending it doesn't happen isn't healthy for young people."

What constitutes healthy sexual practice is subject to debate. Masturbation can be important to those who have lost a spouse by death and to others, including marriage partners. Ignorance regarding the physiology of the body and expected sexual response troubles some marriages. Sex is a strong, human appetite, which God gave creation for the purpose of populating the world. Sex is not the forbidden fruit of Eden. This erroneous belief causes conflict that damages a marriage. Worse still, this and other sexual thought distortions sometimes produce mental illness and aberrations of behavior. Spirituality and sexuality are interdependent. When the human mind separates or suppresses either facet of the personality, man becomes alienated from God. Rather than accepting God's gifts as good, mankind may call good bad and bad good.

Discipline over our bodies; respect for others; and cautious, careful use of sexuality would make for a better, happier society and world. Society needs sexual sanity to disarm pornography and prevent sexual perversions that cause great suffering for the victims—those afflicted and those they afflict.

July journal entry: *Lord, deliver them and me from our loneliness and our desires that burden us. Guide us to healthy outlets for our appetites; satisfy our needs according to your abundance, your wisdom, and your will.*

I long for the peace and joy of death and being with you, God. To be free of the burden of life and its requirements seems desirable. I trust death for Don was good. I know, Lord, you love him more than I ever could.

Forgive me, Lord, for wanting to be with you, when you have left me here for your reasons. You know the road ahead of me and its pitfalls and the suffering I must bear.

Lord, I know you will walk with me. You have promised. I trust you to deliver me from the snares so that finally I may arrive with you, wherever we are going.

While pain of grief threatened to undo my faith, physical desire made me vulnerable to depression and rebellion. I talked to Dr. Somers about my struggle. He asked if there were not someone in my life with whom I could be sexual. I wondered if that was his way of having me explore my true feelings. My true feelings made such a solution untenable. Before Don's death, I thought I would not marry again if he died. Now, I still needed to love and to be loved. I wanted to be married. I missed the rhythm of marriage, even washing a man's clothes. I missed expressing my affection by word and touch. I was addicted to touching and being touched, for even with the release of orgasm, skin hunger is not satisfied. Nevertheless, love of Christ constrained me from a physical relationship outside of marriage.

Questioning my feelings, I wondered if I were strange and wicked to want to be married, with Don not yet dead a year. Many women, widowed like myself, said they would never consider marrying again. Some spoke of remaining loyal to the memory of their mates. Others were sure they could never find another to compare with the husband they once had. Some said they would appreciate having a dinner companion but did not want a physical relationship. Others felt that even going to dinner with a person of the opposite gender would make them feel guilty of unfaithfulness.

Marriage is an earthly institution and I longed for a total physical relationship with someone I loved. Man and woman were made by God for marriage, which God instituted when he created Eve to be Adam's companion and helpmate.

Even in first grade, we had "sweethearts." Male-female interactions go on from the beginning to the end of life. I suppose the fact that I had been a popular young girl made me expect there to be someone for me now. I wanted a special man to come into my life and fill the emptiness left by Don. I did not expect him to be like Don. I was ambivalent about my feelings, but I believed the attraction between man and woman is natural and good.

Orgasm is a natural function of the body. It may occur spontaneously during sleep and is a healthy response of a sound body. Individuals may affect orgasm by masturbation. Appetite and discipline determine whether it is abused or overused. While I no longer attach guilt to my relationship with my body, I act responsibly. Discipline in this area of life, as with other physical activities, i.e., eating, sleeping, exercise, and working, needs to be under the control of my mind and in harmony with my conscience.

Physical desire is not wrong. What we do about it may be wrong. We know by the many types of sexual perversion that there is danger inherent in human sexuality. We are accountable to God, who knows our hearts and our intentions, for our sexual choices.

It is my desire that every act of mine should be motivated by love of God, love of others, or love of self.

There will never be another person like Don. I will never be the person I was with him. No one can replace him for the person he was or as my lover. However, my capacity for physical and emotional love did not die when he died. My sexuality is very much a part of the person God created me to be. Incorporated into my personality as warmth, compassion, tenderness, and beauty, I am fortunate to recognize and accept sexuality as good. God charges me to use all I am to honor him; to show my love and respect for him. I do that by my devotion to God and disciplined use of his gifts to me, one of which is my sexuality.

Chapter XVII

Family Relationships

Andy returned home from The Netherlands two days after I arrived home from Europe. He had become anxious—afraid he would not have enough money for his flight back to the states—because the robbery that first night in Amsterdam had depleted his funds. He left his tennis aspirations behind for home and security. He called a friend when he arrived in New York, and the friend picked him up at Raleigh-Durham Airport. I had started to bed when the doorbell rang. When I opened the door and found Andy standing there, I threw my arms around his neck and burst into tears of relief.

I felt less lonely with Andy home, but it was not easy for either of us to share the same space. I resented his not having regular employment, and he resented his dependence on me. He had a degree in education and had a few opportunities to substitute teach in the local schools. I knew the economy was not good; the country was going through a period of recession. Nevertheless, I urged him to search for a full-time job, which made him angry. It annoyed me that it seemed he loafed around the house all day. Then at night, he would go out to run and sometimes would not return all night long. I told myself that he was handling his enormous grief in the best way he could. It was an unhappy situation for both of us.

One night, while Andy was out running, I had gone to bed. Knowing I was alone, I began to sob convulsively. Andy came in, heard me, and came into my bedroom and took me into his arms. Generally, our private pain acted like a wall between us. We did not share our tears or our pain often or very well. This was an instance when he comforted me.

On August 31, Andy left the house without telling me where he would be or when he would return. When I had a call at 2 AM to go back to the hospital to take care of my pharmacy responsibility, Andy had not returned. My courage had deserted me. I felt I could not make that trip to Durham alone. I felt like a child again and the darkness and lateness threatened my safety. So, when I saw that my neighbor Merle Sykes still had her light on, I phoned her and asked her to ride with me to Durham.

Andy was not in the house when I returned or when I went to work again later that morning. That afternoon, tired, discouraged, I stopped by my church on the way home and let myself in with Don's trustee key. Alone, I went through the order of worship in the hymnal. A visit late one Christmas Eve—when Don had taken me to church after I came home from work to allow me to participate in the "come and go" Eucharist—came to mind. That bittersweet remembrance made me fall sobbing onto the altar floor. I cried until calm acceptance dried my tears.

My journal entry that night records my struggle with self-doubt:

Where do tears originate? Sometimes I wonder if I really love. Does my selfishness only long for that which benefits me? I do long to be on top of the heap, but I want others to be there, too.

The anger I have felt at Andy has gone out of me. God, I want to love him and others as you love me, and I leave vengeance and judgment to you. When I try to figure everything out, I realize how futile my efforts are. I know it is best to be silent and let you handle my life and circumstances. You speak to his heart.

Andy still had not returned on September 2 when I left at 4:30 PM to drive to Hatteras for a visit with Ruby. I needed her gentle, loving companionship. Her widowhood, since Shanklin's death in 1976, enabled her to better understand my state of mind than other family members possibly could. God had equipped her by her passage to comfort me, and I knew she could and would.

The drive to Wanchese, on Roanoke Island, took five hours, and I decided to stop and spend the night with Aunt Lillian, my mother's only living sister. It had been dark a long while, and Hatteras was 60 miles farther. When I did not find her at her home, I inquired of her neighbor, who told me she was at church. Aunt Lillian welcomed me, as I expected she would. We had a nice evening together.

The next morning, we ate our cereal with orange juice in place of milk. Aunt Lillian did not drink milk. The combination was not bad. I stayed on during the morning and we visited other relatives. After lunch, I continued my familiar trip to Hatteras, made unfamiliar by my aloneness, which was much easier in the daylight and after my visit with Aunt Lillian. An hour or so later, I checked in at Ruby's home. She welcomed me warmly.

I deliberately avoided staying with Kathey and Eddie, thinking my presence might further complicate their relationship, which had become troubled. I think now that my avoidance was a mistake. Grief added a great burden to their marriage. Kathey had not finished grieving for her mother, who died in July 1979, after Kathey had nursed her through her last days of cancer alone in Winston-Salem, with Eddie 450 miles away at Hatteras. Guilt on Eddie's part and resentment on Kathey's may have been part of their conflict. Eddie's loss of his father may have affected his ability to make heroic efforts to save their marriage. My ability to cope was impaired. In this instance, my decision may have been subconscious avoidance rather than consideration for them. Maybe I was simply practicing self-preservation. Perhaps I could not face their conflict and admit my helplessness; I therefore, chose a safe place with Ruby. I visited them and we celebrated Kathey's birthday on September 5, but I was oblivious to anyone's grief but mine.

On my last day at Hatteras, I left Ruby's to take a walk on the beach, which was a short distance from her home. When a squall delayed my walk, I stopped at the Sea Gull Motel, owned and operated by my sister Jo and her husband Carlos, for a cup of coffee and to wait for the storm to pass. After the rain stopped, I walked and wept as the ocean sounds reverberated in my brain. None of my visits with family had helped me from feeling unwanted and unneeded, a stranger in my world. Raindrops began to wash away my tears, and lightning began flashing across the sky. A death by lightening would be a fast way to take me out of this suffering, I thought. It would not be my last death wish in the months that followed.

Journal entry that night:

Even as I think of death, I cling to life. Hope springs up, and I know life must go on for me. Family relationships are changing. With Don gone, my future is uncertain.

His death leaves such a void and affects every other relationship I have. Do I feel this way because I am so unsure? Am I initiating conflicts?

I left Hatteras that Saturday afternoon, stopped by Wanchese again to spend the night with Aunt Lillian's daughter Myrtle, and went to church with her on Sunday. We had lunch together and visited during the afternoon. It was late when I left to return to Chapel Hill.

Sunday night, driving the last stretch from Raleigh to Chapel Hill, I talked to Don about many things. Communication between us had been difficult at times. Our efforts seemed clouded and interrupted by less important matters too many times. Now I talked to him, not knowing whether he heard. However, there were no interruptions. I talked to him about Jo suggesting I stay home from church and wallow in my misery as a means of getting over my grief.

How would I find strength and the will to live the next week, Don, without weekly worship and fellowship? Jo still has Carlos, Don. She does not understand that five months is such a short time in grief's economy.

I wondered if he heard me. I talked from habit and need. God listened.

When I arrived home, Andy was not there. I found no note to tell me whether he had been in and out of the house, if he knew when I was coming home, or what I might expect. He did return later that night and seemed more relaxed. When we ate dinner together the next evening, he seemed more ready to talk. After dinner, he went to play tennis with a friend and I went to choir. I did not ask about his whereabouts or his activities. Like the old song, "I didn't ask, he didn't say, so I don't know."

My journal entries and poetry helped me sort out feelings.

God, I confess that Andy is your responsibility, not mine, and that all I am to do is to praise you and to love him. Moreover, the Scripture says I am to praise you for everything.

Thank you, Lord God, for this grief we bear. Thank you for these adjustments we must make and for the growth that must surely follow.

Poem dated September 8, 1980

Tabulating Days

> One, two, three days away from
> the loss of all I knew or wanted:
> Life with you.
> We spent precious days carelessly with
> many tasks and too many meetings.
> Our activities separated us until
> Just shopping together became special—
> A delightful, rare interlude.
> Too much came between us—
> jobs, friends, church, obligations, tasks.
> Now, you are gone and I am here with
> job, friends, church, obligations, tasks.

Everywhere, all the while, my heart cries:
"Gone! You're gone!"
All is nothing!

Eddie and Kathey came November 12 to see UNC beat Duke 30-21 in football and to attend a wedding in Roxboro, where they once lived and taught school. I understood that coming home was rough for Eddie, for I remembered how I felt my first visit home after Daddy died in 1962. I could relate to Eddie's emotion, but he could not know mine since he had never lost a spouse. Our short visit went well, except I fretted that Andy had not come home to be with us. He was helping a woman friend move.

Journal entry: *Maybe adult children, even when they love one another, do not feel the need to be together—or be best friends. This mother wants her brood to flock together for mutual warmth and support—another idealization life denies me. Total strangers can sometimes provide truer friendship than one's own kin can. We do not discount or disregard the blood tie. It is that sometimes childhood experiences have conditioned us to see one another in outmoded frames of reference, which interferes with true friendships.*

Mine may find themselves friends further along—better friends than now. Maybe not. I can neither dictate nor determine that they will.

My niece, Beth, invited Andy and me to spend Thanksgiving, with her family in Virginia Beach, Virginia. Andy agreed to go with me. I was glad for that and felt fortunate not to be alone when we had trouble finding Beth's home. It is better to be lost with someone.

Beth Williams and her daughters...

Beth had all the trappings of Thanksgiving. If only generations of gray birds, geese maybe, of remembered Thanksgivings had not burdened my heart. I appreciated the distraction the visit afforded us and her generosity in including us. If only I could have felt truly thankful.

On December 19, I drove to Greensboro to meet Mona and her daughter-in-law, Pam. We were to share holiday fare with Margie, my oldest sister, and Curt, her husband. I had visited them several times since Don's death the previous April but had not been to Winston-Salem to see Mona. I did not go to Winston-Salem until March. It may have been avoidance on my part, the dread of seeing where Don died.

Grief is inherent in a loss of any kind. I did not have a monopoly on grief. I only felt as though I did. Margie had her personal grief. Many years before, multiple sclerosis had attacked her body. Her grief had been intense and her discouragement devastating. It took time for her to accept that she would never again be as physically able and active as she had once been.

After a visit with Margie...

Margie and Curt gave me emotional support, as they always had and could. I found purpose and appreciation when I visited them. They needed me and I needed them. Their gentle concern and sympathy helped me, and I suppose my visits helped them by giving them someone to share their day.

Approaching Christmas 1980, I wrote:

> In a changing world,
> My life in transition,
> One thing changes not:
> God's mercy and love.
>
> Sons grown, husband gone—
> How different life is.
> Only one thing is sure:
> God's mercy and love.

Moreover, I reflected that the miracle of Christmas is always new and should be free of grief, strife, and pain. Nevertheless, Christmas without Don, who loved trimming the tree and selling Christmas trees for our church, seemed dull and colorless to me. My heart was not in the celebration. Holidays are not joyful for those who grieve and are alone. However, joining the sales force at Amity United Methodist Church to sell the Christmas trees improved my mood. Being with the others and greeting those who came to buy helped me to get beyond the bounds of self. It was a relief to be free of self-pity for a few hours.

Jo invited Andy and me to come to Hatteras for Christmas. When Andy said he would not go, I thought that I should stay in Chapel Hill with him. However, I reconsidered, for he spent little time home with me. So, I decided to make the trip for my own sake. Eddie and Kathey would be at Hatteras, and maybe I should plan to stay with them.

Therefore, on December 23, I left Chapel Hill to drive the lonely trip. Between Columbia and the Alligator River Bridge, pines lined the banks on either side of the canals of the road and the highway stretched in front of me like a long black ribbon. The moon, riding a gray cloud in the night sky, gave some illumination. With music and thoughts of Don to keep me company, I felt at peace and contented, wondering if Don's spirit had defied death to ride with me. God had provided all the beauty of the night for me, and there were no other cars on the road.

I crossed the Alligator River Bridge and then drove nearly fifteen miles farther to Manns Harbor before seeing another car. It had been dark a long while. Again, I decided to stop in Wanchese and spend the night with Aunt Lillian—to go on "home" the next day.

When I arrived in Hatteras the next day, I stopped at Ruby's first. I had a bowl of soup with her and caught up with her news. Then I went to Eddie and Kathey's. They were not at home. In spite of the invitation from Jo, I had entertained the idea of spending this first Christmas without Don with them. They knew that I was coming, but had not left a note. Therefore, when they did not come home in a reasonable time, I took my bags and went to Jo's and Carlos' new home to be the first to enjoy their guest room.

Visit with Jo...

The next day Eddie and I had angry words, for no reason that either of us identified. Unable to talk to him about our misunderstanding, I chafed. Frustration mounted, tempting me to get into my car in the dead of night and drive home to Chapel Hill. Reason overruled emotion. I remembered the old warning: "Don't cut off your nose to spite your face." Leaving would have solved nothing.

My expectations were unrealistic and self-centered, I suppose. Perhaps I expressed myself poorly. I kept running into negative responses. I felt misunderstood and unappreciated by those I loved. I had not yet learned in sessions with Dr. Somers that communication is not the responsibility of one person. I felt insecure and a failure. Incapable of being an instrument of healing to those I loved made me feel ashamed and frustrated. It would be a long time before I would have the resources with which to comfort others. Looking back on those awful days, I know my sons and I hurt one another as we tried to alleviate our own pain. We had to forgive and go on with our lives and our relationships.

Back in Chapel Hill, Cliff arrived February 4, unexpectedly. He had returned to France ten days after the funeral and did not write or call often. I thought he was on the other side of the world. I was so glad to see him, but was troubled that Andy seemed to resent that Cliff came home. I spoke to Dr. Somers about it and he advised, "Do not try to fix it."

On February 7, I had a plumbing problem. Drains needed clearing; I had to purchase groceries; to attend to meaningless, temporal things, as well as to give attention to the all-important relationships of the living. It would have been Don's and my thirty-fourth wedding anniversary. Perhaps the day, as well as the tension between Cliff and Andy, was responsible for the old skin sensations in my arms returning.

On Cliff's last evening at home, February 13, I cooked dinner and we ate together. Andy and Cliff had become reconciled. I was grateful their discord had dissipated. To have them reconciled before Valentine's Day seemed all-important. Valentine's Day underscored my lack of a mate and was hard enough to endure. Of all the special days of the year, it was the worst, following so closely after our anniversary date. Nostalgia and longing filled Valentine's Day. Cliff left to chase tennis fame.

Mona and Margie came to Chapel Hill to see me for my birthday in January. While I had visited Margie and Curt in Greensboro, I had not been to visit Mona in Winston-Salem since Don's death.

Virgil had been the one Mona called when she found Don dead that morning the year before. Virgil spared Mona the call to me and came with her to see me that first afternoon. He attended Don's funeral with Mona, although they had divorced after 26 years of marriage. They cared for one another and for me. In spite of the divorce, Mona's grief was not final and she understood my loss from the perspective of hers. We had a good visit.

Ruby had found a new love, her former pastor, and they were to be married on April 18, the first anniversary of Don's death. Beth Skakle flew from Massachusetts to attend the wedding with me. She and her first husband had been friends with Don's parents, Stan and Mabel, when the children were very young. Beth adored Don, even before she became his stepmother, after both Poppa and Beth lost their spouses. When I expressed some of the anger I felt as we rode toward Hatteras, she shared her love and wisdom and gently admonished me to let it go. Talking to her helped, even though I was not ready to give up my anger. Not yet! I was still seeing Dr. Somers.

During the wedding ceremony, I lost control and sobbed. Beth shushed me. Someone took my tears to be due to loyalty to my brother. Of course, they were wrong. My tears were for me. To attend a wedding on the anniversary of the death of my husband was more than I could handle. Actually, I rejoiced that Ruby had found a new mate to share her love and her life, but their gift of love to one another made me keenly aware of my impoverishment.

Ruby Austin Moser and Rev. Joseph Moser
April 18, 1981 Wedding Day

By September 1981, Andy and I had healed enough to affirm one another. A note that month from Andy reminded me of a dentist appointment and gave me the number of an eating establishment where he had part-time employment. A note said: *Mother, You look great, I am happy to see. The house looks in order. I am glad that you are doing well. Please continue to take good care of yourself. My love and thoughts are always with you. Your loving son, Andrew*

Ten days later, my note to him read: *Andy dear, Have a good day today.*

I'm proud of you—that you're getting on with your life.

We're tough! We can do all things thru Christ our strength.

Love and peace, And joy!

He responded: *Mother, Thank you for being just like you are. I love you.*

I kept those cherished notes of encouragement. After traveling the uncomfortable, sometimes hazardous road we shared in grief, the oasis of appeasement strengthened us for what would come.

My relationship with Andy was traumatized, possibly because we were under the same roof. He did not want to fail me, nor I to fail him. Nor did others mean to fail me, or I them. Numbed by huge doses of loss, our responses were faulty, but we learned and grew in the process of being. Grief is an all-consuming emotion and can be especially hard on close relationships.

Years earlier, an uncle severed his spine in a work-related accident. He was left paralyzed. His wife, unable to accept what had happened, had a nervous breakdown and became emotionally inaccessible. By a miracle of God's grace, and in spite of the psychiatrist's dire prediction to their children that she might never recover, she did recover and returned home to assume the responsibility for her beloved.

We are fragile people. We do not know how a crisis will affect us. The birth of a defective child, or a disabling injury to one of the partners, may cause the other, who is unable to deal with the unexpected, to walk away—abandon the family. My sons and I lived through the crisis that Don's death caused.

I find it difficult to evaluate my relationships. I only have my perspective. In retrospect and considering that period, I believe my grief affected my associations, especially with those closest to Don and me. Distances, individual difficulties, perplexities, and complexities of our relationships affected our communication. Relationships with other people in our lives exerted pressures and demands on each of us. We did the best we could with the wholeness we had, or lacked! I am grateful for our growth in love and that any alienation or misunderstanding was reconciled and forgiven.

I agree with the quote I read that is attributed to author Dick Innes: "To be hurt without forgiving, crushed without becoming more caring, suffer without growing more sensitive, makes suffering senseless, futile, a tragic loss, the greatest waste of all."

When we choose to let go of the offenses against us, God in his love for us will change our pain into the blessings that he promises. We have only to trust and obey him.

CHAPTER XVIII

Friends in Need

A Cuban-French author, Anais Nin, who lived between 1907-1977, wrote: "Each friend represents a world in us, a world possibly not born until they arrived, and it is only by this meeting that a new world is born."

Many friends helped me and in diverse ways. Some listened. Others spoke words I needed to hear. There were those who helped simply because they were themselves and available to me. Many unexpected people made single invitations for a meal; and there were those, closer to me, who continued to be attentive, providing companionship far beyond the first days of loss. All friendships were gifts that breached the huge chasm between being a married woman and singleness. The relationships and shared experiences filled the empty days and helped me to adapt to my new status. They helped launch me onto the Single Sea. Only you who have lost your dearest friend on Earth can understand how unsure I felt and how significant friends' attention was in helping me to discover and accept my new identity as a widow.

Being single meant never being a couple. There were new rules to learn. Activities were now like Solitaire, instead of Bridge. A game with a partner is very different from one you play alone. There were activities with my church family, and my small group was supportive. Kindnesses humbled me. Those who had sustained the deep pain of loss—of child, spouse, parent, or friend—were sensitive to mine. I shared a meal with a young family who had lost an infant. I talked to those who had lost spouses through death, and those who had known divorce also gave me support and comfort. It helped to know how they dealt with their losses. I welcomed directions for a route through the uneven terrain of grief.

Gradually, as invitations dwindled, I had to accept responsibility for planning my route and finding outlets for my individuality. My loneliness drove me like a cattle herder. I hated being at home. One incident made me realize how driven I had become:

A young couple, Karen and Jim Hobbs, invited me to go home with them from church one Sunday. Jim and I sang in the choir. Karen had prepared a delicious meal to share with her visiting parents and me. After lunch, as we sat talking, I began to fall asleep in spite of myself. Karen invited me to use her bedroom to take a nap, and I did. I could not have safely driven the two or three miles to get home. I was exhausted; and even though I had never visited their home before, I accepted the invitation to nap. I did not awaken until 4 o'clock. Then, I quickly tried to cover my embarrassment by expressions of gratitude, apologies, and a quick exit.

As I drove home from Karen and Jim's, I decided I must be intentional about planning for adequate rest and sleep. No doubt remained that I needed more sleep. Yet, never good about going to bed, I found that since Don's death bedtime had become the hardest part of the day, second only to waking up alone.

One Sunday evening, I stopped for an impromptu visit with dear friends, Closs and Fred Wardlaw, and found unexpected comfort and affirmation. They shared a simple meal with me. Then we sat in a darkened room to watch TV. With a Wardlaw on each side of me, sharing a knee covering, we watched without speaking. I felt contented, loved and protected.

I had given up watching TV alone. When Don was alive, football monopolized our living room on Sunday afternoons and Monday evenings in the fall. I read, while Don watched the game.

One evening after Don's death, I turned on a TV football game for the comfort of the familiar sound.

Loyal friends, Mike and Margaret Ronman, fed me any number of meals. They were available to me, and their love sustained me on numerous occasions. I could drop in unannounced, knowing they were there for me. Their steady predictability and familiar foibles, different from my own, gave me great comfort.

A new friend, who came into my life in July, became a special blessing. An old acquaintance reappeared to become a friend indeed. Friends at Durham County Hospital, and Gerald Stahl, the director of the pharmacy department, lent their strength and aid by small acts of kindness. The book Mr. Stahl loaned me, about the land that had nurtured my forbearers for generations, came at just the right time. Unexpectedly, it strengthened my flagging courage. It was as if my father and mother were at my elbow saying: "You can do it, Sybil. We know you can."

Then Nancy Ray reappeared. I had known Nancy through my son Eddie when both our families had been complete. She, her husband, and daughter were neighbors to Don and me and our three sons. However, I did not meet her until she was a patient at Watts Hospital in the early part of my hospital career, around 1965. She had been so ill that I never expected to see her leave the hospital ward. After she came home, we saw one another now and again. Nancy moved away for several years after her husband died, and I heard through friends that she was experiencing very difficult times. Her arrival on my doorstep took me by surprise. I did not know she had moved back into her home on Barclay Road. Nancy helped me in unexpected ways. Sometimes I laughed. Sometimes her efforts to cheer me up puzzled me. Her devotion and loyalty made me grateful.

One Sunday afternoon I saw Nancy coming up my walk. Exhausted and depressed, I did not want to see her or anyone else. I suggested that she come back another day, explaining my weariness. She disregarded my words. She was persistent. "I need money," she said. "Let me clean your house while you take a nap."

My house needed cleaning. Nancy loved cleaning and did it well. So, while she vacuumed, scrubbed, and waxed, I took a nap. Nancy was my angel unawares! What a boon her visit proved to be.

"Your lawn needs mowing," she said. "I'll come mow your lawn tomorrow."

"Okay, Nancy, you can mow my lawn, but don't come too early," I begged.

The next morning, the sound of the lawn mower awakened me. I looked outside to see Nancy, in a yellow slicker, mowing in the rain.

When Christmas came, I had no heart to put up a Christmas tree without Don. That had been his job while I did Christmas cards. I had deliberately not bought a tree from our church. However, Nancy was determined I was to have a tree and showed up with a cedar tree she had cut in the woods. She was pleased with her success and the five dollars I gave her for the tree.

Joyce Dixon is a friend with whom I feel soul to soul. She and her family were part of our lives for many years, when our children were young. We first met when she brought her twelve-year-old son Tommy for tennis lessons with Don. While Don taught Tommy, Joyce and I hit balls to each other and talked about God's love. "God so loved, he gave!" she said.

God loved us when he put Joyce Dixon and her family into our lives. No Christmas was complete without dinner at their home. She was famous for the chocolate-chip cookies, as generous in size as her heart, she made for the tennis team members after Tommy became one of them. She blessed others by her gentle, loving intelligence.

After Tommy joined the Carolina tennis team, Joyce and Tom entertained the team at their home on the alternate years when Carolina played State at Raleigh. I was always part of that party. We gathered at the Dixons' after a Carolina victory over State for their warm hospitality and the delicious food Joyce and Tom had prepared.

"Joyce, why did he call you Mousey?" I asked, after overhearing someone address her with that strange name.

"Oh, Tommy started that," she laughed good-naturedly. "The boys called the maid of one of Tommy's friends "The Mouse." So, Tommy began calling me "Mousey." I rather admired the maid, so I didn't mind."

Many people still tell me how highly they regarded Don. It pleases me to know of their affection for him. However, "like apples of gold in pictures of silver" (Proverbs 25:11), it was Joyce's words that acted like a key to the chamber of my heart when she said, "Sybil, dear, I love you so much. I wish I could reach down into your heart and take away the pain."

We knew she could not do that, but her words soothed my seared spirit more than any words of condolence I ever heard. I never doubted Joyce's love and sincerity. She truly cares about others. Prisoners, a young woman looking for a new job, women who have experienced the trauma of mastectomy—all sorts of people—have received her concern. Joyce taught me so much about loving. Watching and listening to her as she interacts with people reminds me of what it means to love others unselfishly.

The Christmas after Don died, Joyce and Tom took me to see "A Christmas Carol" by Charles Dickens, given by Theater in the Woods in Raleigh. It was painful to go without Don, but would have been more painful without them and their silent succor. I probably did not realize they felt a loss too. All used up on my own loss, how could I realize theirs?

After Tom's retirement from employment in Raleigh, he and Joyce went to live on a mountainside in Balsam, North Carolina, where their five children have summer homes nearby. Over the years, I have visited them there. Tom died in 2008, and I am wishing I could be Joyce for Joyce. I share her loss, for he was my friend too.

Anne Mayor was an acquaintance from college days and a friend for many years after events brought her, a young widow with three small children, back to Chapel Hill around 1964. An adventurer,

Anne moved around a lot. I marveled at her bravery when she took her three children and went to Mexico to work. During the years between, say, 1964 and 1980, Anne moved several times, bought and sold several homes, relocated to Annapolis, Maryland, and New York. Yet 1980 found her again in Chapel Hill, trying to find a career she could really enjoy. She trained in nursing and practiced home nursing care in Charlotte, North Carolina, for several years before retirement back to the Chapel Hill area.

Anne listened to me—curled up in a chair in my living room or hers, in the front seat of a car, or over a meal in some restaurant. For hours, we talked. Anne's supportive presence was very important. She knew me well and had known Don and our sons. Through letters and visits, we shared the events of our individual lives. That Anne was available to me at this particular time of my life seemed something of a miracle to me.

I met Mary Sigrist in July 1980, when she came to Andy's yard sale, trying to find diversion from her grief. Her husband had died in June. I invited her into my kitchen to share coffee and grief that day. We walked many miles together after that, helping one another.

Mary grew up in Carrboro, Chapel Hill's close neighbor. She came back to the area from Baltimore, where she sold real estate, to be near her family for support. She claimed me for her friend, and we shared the pain of loss and misunderstanding of family, and searched for safe roads that we might take. We joined a singles club and another Christian singles group. We whiled away long Sunday afternoons visiting her family or mine. She took me to Baltimore, perhaps as a buffer against loneliness, to meet her friends there. We cooked in her kitchen, which had been her chef husband's domain. We talked about our hopes and our fears as we rode along from place to place. "Everything's going to turn out all right," she would conclude, to reassure both of us.

Mary made me laugh. I invited her as my guest to Durham County Hospital's Fourth of July celebration at Eno State Park. She disappeared after we had eaten. When she returned, laughing, she carried two balloons—for our inner children, hers and mine. She bummed a ride for us with a young man on a golf cart. With our balloons, he drove us up the hill before he said, "You'll have to get off now."

Mary later moved back to Baltimore, where she died of a brain tumor. I never stop missing her and being thankful for her—for her devotion, her humor, and her childlike vulnerability that endeared her to my heart.

Dr. Edward Brecht had been a professor at UNC Pharmacy School during my years there. Later he served as dean for an interim of time. Still later he moved to Louisiana to teach, but returned to Chapel Hill to retire in his home on Rosemary Street. He had been a widower for many years. A loyal, kind man, devoted to pharmacy and pharmacists, Ed Brecht became my friend, in spite of himself. When I was a student in UNC Pharmacy School, Ed taught my classes in Material Medici and Quantitative Chemistry. He was a tall, blonde, blue-eyed handsome man in his thirties then. One of my former classmates said: "All of us were a little stuck on Dr. Brecht."

One afternoon, I went to a neighbor's funeral at Walker's Funeral Home. Ed Brecht was there, too. He greeted me, curious as to why I was there. He followed me to my car to offer his condolences for my loss and told me that he and my neighbor had played chess together. "I'll call you and we will go to dinner," he said.

"Thank you," I said. "That would be nice."

His invitation seemed a distant oasis, but it provided hope for a weary, thirsty desert traveler.

We did go to dinner and talked about stock-market investments. He later sponsored me in the investment club, Pharmaceutical Associates, of which I am still a member. I am grateful for all I learned from him, first as a student and, during my grief, as a friend.

It is possible I gave too much credence to his attention to me because I was so desperately lonely. His recognition of me at meetings, being able to sit with him at investment meetings, his cards to me when he traveled, and mine to him, rare phone calls and visits helped me as I struggled for my identity as a single woman. Even if it meant nothing to him, it made me feel a little like myself as a college girl with a crush on her professor. Once he told me that we could not be friends because our interests were too different. We had pharmacy in common, but he seemed repulsed by my devotion to my church.

The last time I saw him in Hillhaven Nursing Home, recovering from a dreadful infection of his foot, he introduced me to the young man who lived in his home. "Sybil is a longtime friend," he said, thereby nullifying his earlier rejection.

I valued Ed as a friend and mentor. He died while I was away on vacation, visiting Cliff in Wisconsin. I wish I knew how his memorial service came to be held at our church. A mutual friend, who is also a member of our church said, "Sybil, I thought you were responsible for that."

In 1981, I gained an unexpected friend at work, Josephine, a nurse whose husband had died suddenly, too. We had been only casual friends before her loss. After her husband's death, we met almost every day for lunch. We needed each other. We shared our loneliness and our work-related frustrations. We shared our hope of finding another husband to share our lives. She was wonderfully sympathetic, an intelligent, good listener and friend. She beat me to the altar by several months, having met a fine widower with two children to share her life and her generous love. She had no children of her own but became a grandmother through her remarriage. Her life was rich and full because she had the courage to look beyond grief and invest her love in another man's welfare and happiness. Josephine knew what she wanted and exactly how I felt.

Nancy and Randy Moore, friends from church, included me in many of their family gatherings. Nancy easily added me to her large family of brothers and sisters. Her joy of life and Randy's benevolent kindness were like lights on the dark, stormy water. As part of my church family, they were always available.

There is another important friend, who is not included here. Her contribution to my life needs more coverage. In fact, it will take pages to tell of our journey together.

Each friend represented his/her world and enriched my life. I trust that my friendship gave value to each of their lives, in the most critical time of mine. Their physical assistance, encouragement, emotional reassurance, loving attention, or financial advice affirmed my worth. God provided for me by the friends who were in my life, or who became a part of it. I marvel at God's care for me through friends. While we never truly assess how God uses us, if we know we have blessed another, we know our lives have power. If another blesses us, we know God's love has touched us through the love he put into the heart of a friend.

CHAPTER XIX

Weeping Water

Six months into therapy, Dr. Somers assured me that I had made much progress. During a May 1981 appointment, he asked me what my goals were for myself. I could not tell him. While he encouraged me, as usual, by listening, he gave me none of the answers I craved. Only God knew what I could expect of my future, and it seemed my connection to God's communication line was faulty. I could not hear him. I did not trust my judgment of others or myself. I understood neither them nor myself. I felt my feelings had been short-circuited.

On a humorous note, I confessed to my journal after that visit with Dr. Somers: *God is Master Electrician! Fizz (as fizzle) it may be! But light soon!*

My friend Shirley Durham invited me to accompany her, beginning May 10, to her childhood home to Weeping Water, Nebraska. I would see parts of America I had not seen before and would learn many valuable lessons. I think the Master Electrician did some important rewiring in the events and experiences of that trip and in the events leading up to the trip.

My emotions were far from stable and dependable, for all I expected them to be. A year since Don's death, my May 6 journal entry told of a lightening of my spirit and of my decision to give all my battles to Jesus, my commander in chief.

When Dot Morris, wife of Allen Morris, who replaced Don as Carolina's tennis coach, invited me to have lunch with her and her parents at Four Corners, an eating establishment on Franklin Street in Chapel Hill, I had an opportunity to test whether or not I could do it. I felt undefined anxiety when I accepted the invitation. However, when I met Dot and her parents, I felt comfortable and at ease. During lunch, I felt compelled to express my concern for her and Allen; and of Allen's need to protect himself from the demands of the expanded program. I do not know if the coach position changed with Morris, or with Sam Paul, who followed him. In any case, the present Carolina tennis coach is no longer required to teach in the physical education program.

Andy told me that evening that his dog had died in the car during the day. Andy had confined Toasty in his car to keep the dog from chasing him the night before and had not remembered to release the dog when he returned home from running. I went to work and Andy slept late. When he went to the car, he found that beautiful, happy, sweet-tempered animal dead from the heat. I cried bitterly. Tears filled Saturday. It seemed floodgates had sprung open. I could not decide why my tears were so plentiful, only that my need to shed them might never be satisfied. Was this progress? Still struggling to define what I should expect from my future, I yielded to tears and to God.

God is too big to be interested in any pettiness. Except for Jesus, the concerns of my life would be lost on God. God is righteous and good. His affections are not broken or perverted as mine are. I will let God lead.

At 3 AM Sunday, I received a call from one of the nursing staff at Durham County General Hospital, asking me to come to the hospital to prepare a Total Protein Nutrition IV solution, which is used when oral nourishment cannot be given. A task that should have been routine for me turned out to be otherwise.

I arrived at the hospital, let myself into the pharmacy, entered the IV room, and assembled the commercially prepared TPN bag and the additives the doctor ordered. Alone and without distraction, I injected the additional medications, one by one, in just the right amounts into the plastic bag. Normally, a technician prepared the TPN, first drawing up the additives in separate syringes. Another pharmacist or I checked the filled syringes before the technician added them. After additives were injected into the TPN and before the intravenous solution left for the nursing unit, the solution was checked again, by a pharmacist, against the original doctor's order.

When the bulging, heavy plastic IV bag began to leak, I lost my self-confidence. One TPN cost more than a hundred dollars, even before the additives, in the 1980 economy. Had I punctured the bag with one of the syringes?

Even though it was 4 AM, I called Donna Wright, the head IV technician and requested she come to mix another for me. God bless her, she came to my rescue. She mixed the TPN without mishap. I checked it and took it to the right floor, then headed home to get as much sleep as possible before time to return for the Sunday shift.

That afternoon, when I returned from work, I was grateful to find Andy home from his tennis tournament. I had been afraid he would not return before I left for the Nebraska trip on Monday. His being on hand enabled me to leave with a freer mind and more settled emotions.

Shirley and I were on the road a little after 5 AM on Monday, May 10. The Sunday morning TPN adventure had depleted my energies, and all I wanted to do was sleep. Morbid drowsiness kept me asleep for most of the drive to Asheville, where we stopped to tour the upper levels of North Carolina's grandest, most-opulent estate—Biltmore House. I stumbled through the gardens and the green houses, with little enthusiasm, before we headed for a motel on the other side of Asheville.

A motion show in Gatlinburg, Tennessee—a simulation of a helicopter ride over narrow river gorges and fast rides on trains and automobiles, which stopped just short of crashing—tormented rather than thrilled me. I will never subject myself to such "entertainment" again. I am a coward. Already squeamish from lack of sleep, that motion show made me nauseous.

We walked through several of the Gatlinburg craft shops without making a purchase. We might have seen the American Historical Wax Museum, Guinness World Records Museum, or Christus Gardens, but our first travel day had grown old. Feeling as I did, I wanted nothing so much as a long rest. As much as I wanted to be otherwise, all I wanted to do was to sleep.

We found a motel at Pigeon Forge, and another nap prepared me for supper. During supper, an entertainer gave us a preview of a show that would be at the Coliseum that evening. We decided that we would go to see a different group, called Rocky Mountain Hayride. Lively music, clogging, and comedy lifted my lethargy a trifle.

We enjoyed waffles for breakfast the next morning at Wagon Wheel; and spent all morning in Pigeon Forge at Silver Dollar City Tennessee. Part of the appeal of Silver Dollar City Tennessee, and other entertainment areas like it, seems to be that people can pretend to be part of another era, another culture. The craftsmen were selling and showing their wares. Many older citizens and school buses loaded with children and mentally compromised young people were there that morning. (Silver Dollar City Tennessee, renamed Dollywood in 1986, is co-owned by country music singer Dolly Parton, along with the Herschend Family Entertainment Corporation.)

Temperatures had plunged during the night, and our train ride was chilly The water rides repelled us. We chose hot coffee and fennel cake and a show at the saloon, away from the wind. After the show, we picked up a few items as we passed by craft shows , on our way to our car, before we headed toward Nashville.

We arrived at the motel where Shirley had made a reservation for us, on Briley Avenue in Nashville, in late afternoon. We planned to see Opryland. However, it was Tuesday and we learned that it would not be open weekdays until later in the month. Therefore, we decided we would see The Upper Room Chapel the next day.

It had been nearly a year since the European trip with Ruby

and the Dunnam group. I called the Dunnam' home and talked to Jerri Dunnam, but I declined her invitation to visit them. I felt it might be an imposition, since I failed to contact them before our trip. Later, I questioned that decision. Even busy, well-known world players need affirmation and affection. Certainly, I have great affection for Jerri and Maxie Dunnam, who had endeared themselves to me on the tour the year before.

After a good breakfast at Shoney's the next morning, we located The Upper Room building on Grand Avenue. We visited The Upper Room museum, which offers permanent displays of religious paintings dating from 1300 to the present, and the Georgian-designed Upper Room Chapel. We were fascinated by the seventeen-foot-wide by eight-foot-high wood-carving by Ernest Pellegrini, fashioned after Leonardo da Vinci's "The Last Supper." Dr. Dunnam was still world editor of The Upper Room devotional, and we were in his office when a man poked his head in the door to tell him that Pope John Paul II and several bystanders had been victims of a shooting in Rome. We prayed with Dr. Dunnam for the pope, for the other victims, and for the one who fired the shots. Soon after, we left the building for the rest of our Nashville tour. Later that day we learned the pope had survived his six-hour operation and the two bystanders did not die.

After leaving The Upper Room building, we walked across the street to what had been Scarritt College campus. Actress Belle Bennett founded Scarritt College in Kansas City, Missouri, in 1891, to train young women missionaries. It moved to Nashville, Tennessee, in 1924 and became Scarritt College for Christian Workers. Scarritt Hall, Bennett Hall, the Tower, and the Chapel, known collectively as the Belle Bennett Memorial, were built between 1924-1927 with funds raised by the Woman's Missionary Societies and the Methodist Episcopal Church South. Shirley and I were interested by reason of the connection to the United Methodist Church, especially the Women's Division. Our local organization programs had mentioned Scarritt in the past.

Scarritt College closed in 1980 and opened as The Scarritt

Graduate School in 1981. Both schools educated and trained students for domestic and international church and community positions and conferred degrees in church music and Christian education. However, the enrollment fell so low that in 1988 Scarritt Graduate School closed. The Women's Division, affiliated with the General Board of Global Ministries of the United Methodist Church, bought the 10 acres of land and buildings. They renovated the buildings and opened Scarritt-Bennett Center, now used for conferences, weddings, and retreats. They welcome a group as large as one hundred-thirty or an individual.

We rode by Vanderbilt University and on to Centennial Park to see the full-size replica of the Parthenon. Its original is located at the Acropolis in Athens, Greece. The replica in Nashville, which was originally built for Tennessee's 1897 Centennial Exposition, is an imposing building and houses Nashville's permanent art collections. We did not feel we had time to look at the art. We were on a schedule in Shirley's mind, since she did not drive after dark. She planned to pull into a motel well before dinnertime.

On an impulse, we left Route 24 to take Route 13 to Carbondale, Illinois, hoping to see a couple who had been members at our church. It was a wild-goose chase, for we did not find them.

The rain, which had begun as we drove, turned into a violent storm. We checked into a Holiday Inn in Carbondale. A blackout occurred after our dinner at the motel restaurant. When the lights were on again, we visited the lounge to enjoy the live music. I had a virgin pina colada.

When we walked into that motel room, I felt sad and impatient. Then unreasonable anger filled my mind. I hated not having my mate to share motel rooms.

Thursday, May 14, we left the Holiday Inn in the rain. My dreams had been disturbing. I awakened to a replay of old hurts and doubts that had haunted me in Europe. The rain and dreariness accentuated my woe.

I read our devotions to Shirley as we rode along. Tears welled up and spilled over, as the lonely road stretched ahead of us. Hoping to dispel my heaviness of spirit by expressing my feelings, even while I felt ashamed of them, I said to Shirley, "I feel so helpless. My life is like a battlefield!"

Discouragement seemed like a betrayal of Christ. I tried to justify my feelings to myself. I had remembered Betty Boling's note about battles that belonged to God and my resolve to let God handle the battles. "Be not afraid nor dismayed. . .for the battle is not yours but God's." II Chronicles 20:15 (KJV)

Here I was, failing to live up to my vow. "Surely, if I remain surrendered, God will win this battle for me," I said.

"Sybil, that doesn't seem quite right to me. You have to fight back."

"I'm tired of fighting. I can't change my feelings. I'm so angry!" I said.

"You can't let it discourage you," Shirley replied.

"Yes, I can!" I declared irritably, spilling more tears. "Yes, I can!" I wanted to scream.

"Don't you see? Sometimes I'm completely immobilized by all this emotion!" I tried to explain.

Quietly, I thought, *Shirley cannot understand my unreasonable anger. Well, neither can I. How could she understand?*

"Shirley thanks. You're a great friend. I know you care."

Indeed, I knew. Shirley invited me to share this trip; gave me her companionship for an extended number of days; made decisions regarding stops, motels and other things. It was wonderful to be relieved of responsibility for the time we traveled together.

Shirley prayed for me, and I drove awhile to relieve her. Both the driving and the prayer helped. As we rode along, we listened to a sermon titled "The Essence of God," which quieted my heart. I recognized my impatience and rebellion and asked God for more of himself to satisfy my soul.

We crossed the Mississippi and Missouri rivers as we rode over straight roads running between both hills and plains. Shirley brought to my attention the dark soil.

Later in the afternoon, in Missouri, the rain finally lifted.

When we crossed into Nebraska, Shirley told me that her state is marked off in square miles by the roads, some of which I could see before me. What contrasts our country holds.

We arrived before dark in Weeping Water at Shirley's childhood home. Her father, Edward Steinkamp, lived with her sister Ruthanne and her husband Carl Tapper. They made me feel very welcome. From my bedroom window, I could see the black soil and the cows, and lots of country.

The next morning I awoke with longing and grief, which I had hoped to leave behind. After breakfast, Shirley and I went to visit her mother in Louisville Care Center and to see Shirley's brother Dale and his wife Audrey. The visit to the Louisville Care Center gave me new ways of evaluating my own life and circumstances.

Shirley's mother, a sweet, patient spirit, who we visited each day we were there, and Shirley's kind, ninety-year-old-plus father, were separated by age and infirmity. It had been necessary for these old lovers to adjust to conditions they did not choose. Many old men and women, some vegetating and waiting to die, were residents with Shirley's mother. Their existence seemed so dreary and hopeless. I thought they would be better off if they were free from their worn-out bodies and minds and present with the Lord.

Then I met Dorothy, a woman bedridden with multiple sclerosis, completely dependent on others at the care center. Yet, Dorothy was cheerful and humble and expressed her gratitude to God. Her illness separated her from her husband. I felt ashamed for not valuing my own health and freedom more; I would be more content.

Between the first days of our arrival and the memorial service the day before we left, we enjoyed much activity. Shirley's friends and family were lovely and generous toward me.

Nebraska is justly proud to have erected its beautiful Capitol in Lincoln without outside help. It is built of white marble, and atop its golden dome a sower scatters corn. The Capitol is a testimony to the dignity and character of Nebraska's people.

Inside the Capitol, mosaic murals and inlaid marble floors depict history and the heritage that makes the people proud.

Surprised by the building's magnificence, I felt such admiration for these, my fellow Americans. I found myself comparing their edifice favorably with St. Peter's in Rome. St. Peter's is bigger, but Nebraska's Capitol is likewise awesome.

That same day we toured the broadcasting offices of "Back to the Bible," which had nurtured my Christian growth through its broadcasts and its literature. And we met Shirley's sister Wanda and had coffee with her and some of her friends. We also did a bit of shopping while we were in Lincoln.

During nights in the safe, small corner room of the Steinkamp homestead, I had many dreams as I slept. Some dreams were full of images I did not understand. I believe dreams are curative, therapeutic. I attempted to keep the disturbing ones from influencing my mood by accepting them as I do a cloudy day or rain, for I believe my dreams are meant to help, not hurt me.

My journal entry May 20 read: *Lord, thank you for a good day. Forgive me when I have doubted your love. This imperfect world is imperfect because man sinned—is still sinning. I have no right to complain.*

When I see Dorothy and other helpless people, I realize how blessed I am. True, I cannot understand their suffering. I do not fully understand how Christ's suffering accomplished so much and continues to change and redeem lives. But, I can trust you and give you thanks.

We went back to Lincoln the next day to visit Shirley's sister Wanda and her husband Charles Gardiner at their home, and to spend the night with them. We arrived before noon, had lunch with Wanda and toured a decorator house. We drove around other areas and came back to meet the Gardiner daughter Linda and her children, a girl and a boy. We all went to Valentino's, for pizza and salad, and then back to the house.

The boy locked Linda's car keys in the car, a bad experience for the little guy. I told him that Jesus loves us even when we make mistakes, for it is by our mistakes that we learn. I identified with his hurt.

That evening we went to see "Mame" by The Little Theater. The cast had fun performing, and we had fun watching.

The next morning before we left, Wanda took us to see her church. Then we picked up Shirley's friend Betty and took her with us to see other friends. We had a nice lunch with Flossie Domingo and her other guest in Louisville and spent the rest of the afternoon playing UNO and King in the Corner card games with them.

That evening, Ruthanne invited their brother Dale, his wife Audrey, and their lovely daughter Sara; and prepared a delicious spaghetti supper. I had chance to talk to Sara, who startled me by confessing she feared she would be unpopular with her peers if she did her best. Even the young have fears and struggles as they adjust to new phases of their lives. Only circumstances differ from one to another.

May 23, the special day that had brought us across the country, arrived. Most of the day Shirley and I spent getting ready for parties related to the 90th Alumni Banquet of Weeping Water High School. It was Shirley's fortieth graduation anniversary. Shirley went to the hairdresser while I stayed at home to do my own. We enjoyed a surprise visit from Shirley's aunt and uncle, who stopped by on their way home to Albuquerque, New Mexico.

Shirley had just finished pasting on artificial fingernails when Wanda and Charles arrived from Lincoln. Charles later drove Shirley and me from the farm into Weeping Water for a pre-banquet party. My name tag read: HELLO! My name is Sybil Skakle—Shirley's friend.

We visited, chatted, and I met new people at the party, where we stayed until time to go to Weeping Water High School. Soon, we moved as a group to the cars and continued our conversations and exchange of information as we rode to the event. The tables were set up in a large area, probably the basketball court, at the school, with each graduating class having a table of its own. Shirley's group was comparably large. I did not mind being an observer and listener as they noted who had not made the party and why. Some had died. Their remembrances, while not mine, were very like mine.

One person attending was the husband of Dorothy of the nursing home, with another woman. Another man I met, recently widowed, flirted with me a bit, which proved to be refreshing and a small affirmation.

Sunday, May 24, Shirley and I attended United Methodist Church of Weeping Water. The pastor's reference to memories of loved ones caused me to cry. His unexpected words had dislodged the scab protecting my raw being.

Ruthanne cooked again, when another female relative entertained us for a great meal and time of fellowship that afternoon. There were twenty-five or thirty at the gathering of family and friends.

Later that afternoon, a childhood friend of Shirley's came to visit. He took us with him to chase hot-air balloons. We watched them land in one of those black fields, and saw two riders disembark from each balloon.

On May 25, I felt deeply grateful for the opportunity to be part of the Memorial Day service at the cemetery. It was touching, patriotic, and meaningful. Relatives had placed flowers on every grave. Flags adorned the graves of those who had served their country in the military.

While the band, dressed in red and white, played marches, uniformed Boy Scouts stood near. Members of the American Legion carried the colors (flags) and fired a salute. The principal of the local elementary school gave a fine address, worthy of a larger place and crowd but certainly not wasted on Americans assembled there. Proud to be an American, my patriotic emotions filled my heart. I felt privileged to be there.

Various churches and groups from the community presented floral tributes for the memorial marker. One little girl, dressed in white, marched staunchly forward between the honor guards, placed the wreath on the grave, and returned to her place with solemnity and purpose.

As we honored the men and women who had given their lives for their country, I remembered that death caused separation for them and their loved ones too. Many hearts like mine have suffered through long, miserable, awful days of grief. The bereaved are unnamed and unappreciated, and we find no more comfort in the floral tributes than the dead do. The battles of soul are as quiet as a graveyard in winter.

On May 26, it was time to say our goodbyes. I had engaged in many sensitive, private emotional skirmishes in that white, two-story house in the country, amidst the cows and emerging corn. For me those goodbyes were highly emotional, for I had come to care deeply for Shirley's family and this place. Dad Steinkamp stood outside the back door, unsteady on his feet. His eyes, which had observed so many changes in ninety-plus years, filled with tears. He kept saying, "My little girl's going to leave me and go back to North Carolina."

We took pictures and lingered to embraces yet again. Then, at 9:30 AM, Shirley and I climbed into her car and waved our last goodbyes to her dad and to Ruthanne and Carl. It was time to begin our eastward journey—time to go home—time to leave Weeping Water, where I left tears and haunting dreams and began to move forward more confidently into my new life.

Shirley Durham,
Dad Stienkamp and Sybil

Weeping Water

Years ago, before the white man came
to Turtle Island,
Two Indian tribes battled in the valley
between two hills.
Many braves died in that bloody, fierce
fight that day.
Squaws and maidens wept in anguish
in camps on opposite hills,
The sound filled the night air
and their tears trickled down the hills.
At the bottom their tears flowed together into
a stream the natives named Weeping Water.
In 1981 I visited Nebraska, mourning
my dead, brave warrior.

Legend says weeping and wailing is heard
beside the falls of Weeping Water Creek
I wonder if the sound is louder since I added my
tears to the flow.

CHAPTER XX

Peace in the East

By three o'clock, Shirley and I had arrived in Amana, Iowa, after a nice traveling day and lunch in Des Moines. We checked into Colony Inn and did a bit of shopping before supper.

After we had eaten, we went to a lounge in the motel next door to listen to live music. Steve Bledsoe led the group. We stayed late and got to know and like Carrie Lou Gill's singing voice and her drumming, but I never heard of either of them again.

Neither Shirley nor I slept well that night. My dreams were bizarre, and the room was too warm for Shirley. We decided that perhaps we were anxious about returning home.

The next morning we ate breakfast near our motel before taking the grand, four-hour tour of Amana. We did not want to miss anything. Along the way, we enjoyed the clean, interesting shops. I picked up a decorative oak cutting board as a wedding gift, and enough lovely wool material to sew two skirts.

We learned that the Amana Colonies was founded in Germany in 1714, as the Ebenezer Society, or the Community of True Inspiration, to protest arbitrary rule of church and state. They moved to America in 1843 to escape unfriendly government and high rents. Led by Christian Metz, they first settled near Buffalo in Erie County, New York. Seven communities comprised the colonies. They had their own mills and factories, tilled the soil, and formally accepted communism and communal living as their way of life.

In 1855, when the expansion of Buffalo threatened their isolation, approximately fifteen hundred of the Inspirationists moved to the frontier state of Iowa and located in Iowa County. They incorporated as Amana Society to continue their community life of "brothers all." For nearly a century, they conducted a successful experiment in communism, inhabiting seven villages and owning twenty-six thousand acres of land.

In 1932, by a unanimous vote, after old idealism and spiritual enthusiasm had waned, Amana Society reorganized, based on cooperative capitalism, as a joint stock company. The owners and employees are its stockholders.

While we saw a large white Amana manufacturing building in the distance, we chose the history and culture of Amana. Instead of Amana meaning ranges, refrigerators, washing machines, and dryers, Amana became, for us, the name of a people and a quaint village with an amazing history.

Coffee and pastries revived us before the tour of a museum, and we left Amana around two o'clock to drive seven hours, to arrive at Danville, Illinois, near the Indiana border. Redwood Inn, where we stayed, looked like a Swiss chalet, and there we found brass beds! After supper, we visited the lounge to listen to the music. I got to dance a couple of times and had an experience that furthered my education of being single. When my dancing partner, Bob, suggested we couple, I had to decide how to handle myself. I told him that I belonged to Christ and was interested only in a lasting relationship with total commitment.

"That is the way it ought to be," he said.

I expressed my appreciation for having an opportunity to dance and thanked him sincerely. Thereafter, he asked neither me, nor anyone else, to dance. He still stood at the bar when we left the lounge at 11 PM.

Guilt attacked me. Had our being in the lounge been inappropriate for a couple of women? Perhaps Bob misunderstood our reasons for being there. Christ had been misunderstood when he accepted an invitation to eat with tax collectors. As a Christian, I am responsible for having well-established limits within my loyalty to Christ, and for my intentions when I visit a questionable place. However, Christ died for those who go for the wrong reasons and without acknowledging God's authority in their lives. While we danced, I reminded Bob of God's kindness and mercy.

From Danville, I called a friend in Veedersburg, Indiana— Betty Neushafer, whom I met when she visited in Hatteras in 1956-57. She, her husband, and another couple stayed in one of my parents' rental apartments for a week. Since then, Betty had been a true, wise friend. Whenever I faced a problem about which I wanted loving, Christian counsel, based on biblical references and wisdom, I wrote to Betty for advice. She never failed to respond promptly—to share her thought and opinion about what the mind of Christ would be for my decision. I trusted her and relied on her, although we had not seen each other for many years. Both she and I had lost many people we loved—my parents, her husband, my husband.

My trust of Betty had been established when she and I shared an experience in ministry when I first knew her. I asked Betty to talk to Celia, who lived in one of the rental apartments, for one day I discovered Celia lying on the couch in the apartment with a Bible open on her breast, looking for answers to the unreasonable fear that kept her a prisoner. Agoraphobia is a morbid fear of being in open places. I did not have enough confidence in God or myself at that time to confront Celia's captivity. Betty did. With Celia between us, we led her down the hall of the apartment house, assuring her of God's love and understanding. We told her about Christ's love and prayed for her release from her phobia.

Celia's need had united Betty and me that summer afternoon in Hatteras many years before.

After Celia and her Navy Seabee husband returned to California, Celia wrote to tell me that she had found healing and freedom in Christ. Our prayers were answered for Celia!

Shirley and I arrived at Betty's apartment with little trouble. Her daughter Barbara joined us for breakfast. We had a good visit and shared devotions and prayers before resuming our trip.

After leaving Betty and Barbara, Shirley and I drove on a route along the Ohio River, which took us through many small towns. Shirley drove until Huntington, West Virginia. Then I drove to Beckley, where we checked into our motel before going to supper at Sir Robert Supper Club, which had a band and stage show. I enjoyed Alaskan crab legs and the show—until the second song. "Smoke Gets in Your Eyes" brought memories and tears.

I remembered that I had invited Don and some of his friends to our dorm dance at the University of North Carolina, where I came as a transfer student the fall before, and he had just enrolled, recently out of the United States Coast Guard, to go to school on benefits of the G.I. Bill. I bought a black net evening gown, with a big sweetheart rose at the waist, to wear to the dance to impress Don. One shoulder was bare. I felt beautiful. We danced for the first time together to "Smoke Gets in Your Eyes," that evening. I felt lighthearted. Don complimented my dancing. That was wonderful!

My response to the song prompted this journal entry:

Lord, I really am still having trouble sorting it all out. Shirley tells me that I can. I try. I do! I know I must find courage, determination, and the secret of putting the past behind me. The problem seems to be, partially at least, in the mixture of bitterness and beauty. How can I consistently manage to separate them—keep the beauty and discard the bitterness that undermines my peace?

I know you are taking care of it, but am I doing my part? Am I?

We left Beckley the next morning after breakfast. We drove until Winston-Salem, North Carolina, and stopped at Mona's for a sandwich and a visit with her. We arrived in Chapel Hill at 3:30 PM on the afternoon of May 29, 1981. When I arrived at my home, Andy was getting ready to leave for Richmond, Virginia.

After a busy afternoon and evening doing my coming-home chores, I wrote in my journal:

I'm trying to do as Shirley kept saying, "Don't look back."

I need to go forward. Okay, Lord, let's go for broke! You are my all-in-all. Yet I've been acting like you're incidental. Forgive me.

I cannot truly fathom your love being more than any other love. So lonely have I been for the physical love and presence of my husband that I have lost sight of your right to the earth and all that are part of earth. How do I get to a place of acceptance?

I still have trouble not idolizing Don. That was wrong when he lived and is more wrong now than ever, maybe.

God, we have been told that you are alive and each of us lives and dies unto you! So be it! Lord, teach me in quietness of meditation, in my everyday affairs, what I need to know. Protect my dreams as I sleep. Thanks!

Home again, I began to follow the rhythm of my life, built around work, home, church, friends, and family. Something had changed, however. The background music of my life seemed happier.

Surrounded by neglected chores and the accumulation of tasks due to vacation, one morning I felt especially energized rather than overwhelmed. Since Don's death the garden and yard, which I normally enjoyed, had held no allure for me. That morning, I felt an urgency to go outside to work.

I thought of Shirley's words, "You have to fight back." I opened the closet door, collected my garden gloves stored there, and slipped them onto my hands. After finding the garden tools in the outdoor shop, I began to take charge.

It felt good to be outside. Like a sudden raindrop, that

Scripture Betty Boling had sent to me in a note came to mind: *Thus says the Lord to you: "Do not be afraid or dismayed because of this great multitude, for the battle is not yours, but God's."* 2 Chronicles 20:15 (NKJV)

I actually chortled as I spoke aloud: *Okay, God, You take care of the battle and I'll take care of the battlefield.* Pulling at the overgrowth, clipping the hedges made me sweat with exertion as this "battlefield" yielded to my efforts. A desire for weed-free flowerbeds fired my imagination. Hope and joy welled up in my heart and in my spirit. I felt capable of disciplining the hedges. I felt truly free of grief's shackles; free to accomplish whatever I wanted to do.

Grief is never completely over, because we have memory. However, my grief had changed. It no longer ruled all my days. More days were good ones than not. Physical exercise and involvement helps to dispel depression and clears the way for the Lord to win the battle. Taking responsibility for myself, remaining loyal to God's authority in my life, I had begun to let grief go.

Now I knew that I could choose my mood; that negative emotions yield to prayer, that physical exercise reduces stress, that sleep normally cures fatigue, and that healing is progressive. Grief had wounded me to the depths of my soul and spirit, but God never left me alone, and he never will. God wins battles of the ages and my small affrays, when I let him. Grief enlarged my soul and gave me a new understanding of others who grieve. I became a better, more-compassionate person, as the book I hated claimed I would.

God promises joy in the morning. He built hope and resurrection into the cycle of our lives. Grief has its season, but seasons change. I look forward to reunion with those I love, because God loves me and has promised that through his son I have this privilege.

A Happy Day
May 17, 1982
Mona and Bill Hunter's Wedding Day

"A picture is worth a thousand words."

2007 Thanksgiving Gathering of the Skakle Family at Hatteras

A generation has passed since this grief story began, with the death of a husband and father. Our seven grandchildren are the rising generation and I am the matriarch of the Skakle Family.

When we gathered for Thanksgiving at Dare Dreamer, the house we dreamed about for years before it became a reality in 2001, only Eddie's three daughters – Faye, Snow and Brooke- were missing from the picture.

It seems that I have lived a lifetime since 1980, when this story began. I married again in 1983, divorced in 1990 and married again in 1991. That husband died of cancer nine months later.

I retired from pharmacy in 1990 and since then have kept busy writing and with other activities. God has been with us in the storms and in the bright days.

Thank you for sharing our story.

Sybil A. Skakle
Skakle@att.net, or sybilskakle@juno.com